Introducing Sector Rotation

4th Edition

Tony Pow

Why you want to read this book

Obviously this book has been rated by my competitors. Most if not all have one or two strategies (I have 21) and their authors have not made the same performance as mine (talking is different from actual investing). I believe it is the best book for the topic. Check out the table of contents to start. Order it and return it (check Amazon's return policy) if it does not fit your needs. As of 5/2020 I bet that no author besides me made over **4 times** using sector rotation starting the amount more than my annual salary then..

- My annuity has grown **four** times using sector rotation. I started with a position more than my annual salary then, and hence I do not boast with a tiny amount. In March, 2000, I switched out all my tech positions from this account. How many authors can say that? We can make money by spotting the market plunge and spotting the trend.

- As of 9/25/15, I glanced through my competing books in Kindle format. Here are my personal comments and check whether it makes sense to you.

  - ETF Rotation. 3.5 stars. **91** pages. $9.99.
  - Super Sectors. 3.5 stars. 264 pages. $26.39.
  - Profiting from ETF Rotation. 3.5 stars. **35** pages. $7.55. Must be reviewed by friends or it is very, very concisely great.
  - Standard & Poor's Sector Investing. 3 stars. 260 pages **$97.58**.
  - Dual Momentum Investing. 5 stars. 240 pages. $34.99. After reading several of the comments and the table of contents, I only found only one chapter is useful to me. The absolute momentum and relative momentum have been described in my book.

  This book has about 90 pages (solid information and nothing on my life to fill the pages) and the Kindle version only costs $4.99.

My motivation to write this book is sharing my experiences, both bad and good. I provide simple-to-follow techniques using the free (or low-cost) resources available to us. I have been successful in investing for decades. I am enjoying a comfortable financial life. I do not hold back my 'secrets' as my children are not interested in investing. It is my small legacy in sharing my investing ideas.

If you are looking how to make 100% return overnight, there are many other books claiming to do so and this book is not for you.

This book describes how to be a 'turtle' investor making fortune gradually and surely. As everything in life, there is no guarantee this book will make you money. However, the chance of success will be substantially improved especially when you practice on most of the ideas presented in this book.

Click the link for the articles I wrote for SeekingAlpha.com, a site for investors. http://seekingalpha.com/author/tony-pow/articles

Andrew, a contributor on Sector Rotation article at Seeking Alpha, said, "Great stuff, Tony. It's great to meet experienced traders such as yourself. I had a browse through the book and think your method is a little more refined than mine." The current version included "Momentum Strategy" adding about 30 pages.

Why you trust me

All of the below are provable. I did made some blunders and both are described in this book.

- My annuity (not recommended due to my higher tax bracket during retirement) grows to **5** times mostly using Fidelity's funds for sector rotation.
- My simple technique that does not use chart told us to **exit the market** on around March 20, 2022.
- I switched most (all in my annuity) of my tech funds to other sectors (should be cash if I had a time machine) in April, 2000. It was only provable if Fidelity keeps record for the year 2000.
- I achieved 80% return in my largest taxable account in 2009.
- I recommended to buy oil when it was $30 at Seeking Alpha, a website for investors.
- I recommended 20 stocks in an article Amazing Return in Seeking Alpha. If you bought them on the published date, you would have beaten the S&P 500 index by over 100% without considering dividends as demonstrated in my other article A Tale of Two Portfolios. Search these articles.

I challenge anyone who had better one-year performance for recommending a diversified portfolio of 15 or more stocks.

Contents

Introduction

Sector rotation has been proven to make good profits with the least risk if it is properly implemented. However, sectors are risky, less diversified and more volatile than the market. This book describes 21 strategies from the simplest sector rotation for beginners to advanced sector rotations for experts. Most other similar books have only one strategy. As of 5/2020, my annuity account (not too many choices while working for a mutual fund company) appreciates more than **4 times** using sector rotation starting with the amount more than my yearly salary then. When you correctly choose the right strategy from my 21, you should make good money. In addition, you can combine several strategies such as the year-end strategy and market timing. In the long run, this book improves your odds in making profits over traditional schemes in sector rotation by:

- Market Timing. When the market is plunging, do not buy any stock including sector ETFs and sector funds. This book provides a simple chart to detect market plunges. The simplest (for beginners) is a sector rotation between SPY (an ETF that simulates the market) and cash (or an ETF of short-term bonds).

- The next rotation strategy involves four ETFs in a rising market. Optionally, advance investors can include a contra ETF to time the market further. Buy the best performer from the last month of these four selected ETFs.

- Some sectors perform better in different stages of a market cycle.

- Many free sites describe the best sector performers such as Seeking Alpha.com and CNNfn.com.

- Evaluate sectors using Technical Analysis (simple charts available free from the web) and Fundamental Analysis.

- You should spend one or two hours a month to determine which sector to rotate to, or move your portfolio to cash when the market is risky. The "Buy and hold" strategy has not performed since 2000.

- I have not tested out all the strategies (as I have a life too), but they have to be proven profitable by someone at least in one market condition. We have to match the strategy or strategies to the current market. For example, the strategy should have a high chance of success if the market is trending up and the stock has high insider purchases. **Consult your investing advisor before committing any money.**

Links from YouTube
Simple sector rotation, another one, and one more.
https://www.youtube.com/watch?v=85IRL__3oR8&t=219s
https://www.youtube.com/watch?v=gu-46zcBwsl&t=177s
https://www.youtube.com/watch?v=acOMOh7Zc6c
How to use this book

Do not trade the stocks discussed in this book, as they may be outdated. Learn the reasons they are recommended.

This book is not a novel that you should read sequentially. This book is organized as a reference book. You can start any chapter or find the related topic as needed. I recommend starting to glance at the table of contents if available.

Most graphs and tables are in landscape orientation (recommended for small screens) for both paperback and e-readers. Some graphs may not be displayed adequately on a small screen of an e-reader.

Use a PC to read the graphs on the larger screen. For better orientation, just flip your e-reader device 90 degrees if it is available. Most e-readers let you select a table or a graph to display it to fit the screen.

The **font size** (Ctrl Minus for browser implementation of e-readers) should be adjustable for e-books.

There are clickable links to web articles and/or YouTube videos, which are usually more entertaining. Most of them are from public websites such as Wikipedia. Some public links may not be available in the future as they are not under my control and my book may change. For security, get the information such as "RSI(14)" directly from the source; the primary ones are Wikipedia, Investopedia, YouTube and Fidelity.

These links extend the usefulness of this book by making available specific topics that may not be interesting to every reader. It also provides articles (most are not written by me) for more in-depth analysis. Instead of typing the links to your browser, you can access the following website to access most of the links easier. One reader commented, "(the links have) lots of useful information. The author also has a sense of humor."
http://tonyp4idea.blogspot.com/2021/05/web-links-for-printed-copy-of-my-book.html

Fidelity provides video clips to explain some of the basic terms. Fidelity does not require a balance to open an account; I have no affiliation with them except I retired from Fidelity. Take advantage of their extensive research and info. YouTube offers similar video lessons. This book provides many of the links for the paperback readers. In any case, get the same information or extra information by entering a search in Wikipedia and/or Investopedia (http://www.investopedia.com/) such as "Dogs of the Dow".

'Afterthoughts' includes my additional comments and ideas of minor importance. There are fillers with tips, refreshing pictures (most were taken by me) and jokes (most original) to fill up some empty space of the printed book. Fillers, links and afterthoughts should not disrupt the flow of reading this book. One user commented on my fillers: "Thanks for the jabs (Fillers) to make the reading fun while getting an education".

For convenience, this book uses SPY, an Exchange Traded Fund (ETF) simulating the S&P 500, as the benchmark for the market.

Since most of the stock recommendations are probably obsolete by the time you read about them, use them as examples and do not trade the mentioned stocks without consulting your financial advisor first. For simplicity, I treat ETN the same as ETF.

About the author

I graduated from Cal. State University at San Jose in Industrial Engineering and University of Mass. in Amherst with a MS in Industrial Engineering. I have retired from a job in IT at Fidelity and I have been an investor for over 30 years.

Dedication

To all retail investors and future retail investors including my grandchildren. I sincerely hope this book will build bridges with fellow investors with different backgrounds, as you can continue to learn about investing / trading. Also, this book is dedicated to all support staff during the pandemic of 2020.

Acknowledgement Thanks to all free websites.

Important Notice
© 2021-2025 Tony Pow. Emails to pow_tony@yahoo.com.

Version	Date
Edition 1.0	01/2021
1.4	01/2025

Book store managers can order the printed version of this book from Createspace.com.

Disclaimer
Do not gamble with money that you cannot afford to lose. Past performance is a guideline and is not necessarily indicative of future results. All information is believed to be accurate, but there is not a

guarantee. All the strategies including charts to detect market plunges described have no guarantee that they will make money and they may lose money. Do not trade without doing due diligence and be warned that most data may be obsolete. All my articles and the associated data are for informational and illustration purposes only. I'm not a professional investment counselor, a tax professional or any other field. Seek one before you make any investment decisions. Remember to consult with a registered financial adviser before making any investment decisions. The above mentioned also applies for all other advice such as on accounting, taxes, health and any topic mentioned in this book. Tax laws change all the time, so talk to your tax advisors before taking any action. Some articles may offend some one or some organization unintentionally. If I did, I'm sorry about that. I am politically and religiously neutral. I have provided my best efforts to ensure the accuracy of my articles. Data also from different sources was believed to be accurate. However, there is no guarantee that they are accurate and suitable for the current market conditions and /or your individual situations. The values of some parameters such as RSI(14) are arbitrarily set by me. My publisher and I are not liable for any damages in using this book or its contents.

How the rate of return is calculated

They are for education purposes only, and do not make your investing decisions based on them. I usually use annualized for better comparisons; 4% in a month is more than 5% in a year for example. For short-term strategies including momentum, shorting and year-end strategy, I use the returns for a month, and sometimes including returns for 2 months for comparison. Annualized returns are usually used for long-term strategies. The holding periods may have a few days off due to holidays and weekends. For simplicity, most of my returns do not include commissions, exchange fees, order spread and dividends. Most numbers have been rounded up for better readability. The return = profit / investment. I and my publisher are not liable for any error.

Section I: Basic sector rotation

1   Sector rotation in a nutshell

How to start

I have been rotating sectors in my annuity investments for quite a long time with a sum of more than my annual salary at the time. As of 1/2020, it had increased about four times. My mutual fund employer had a lot of restrictions for me trading stocks, so rotating sector funds in my annuity was the best investment tool for me.

For a starter, I recommend that you paper trade your strategy first. Use Finviz.com, SeekingAlpha.com and/or Fidelity.com to select the best performing sector and/or use my quick analysis of ETFs. Switch it every month (or two) to the ETF corresponding to the best sector. Again, switch to cash when the market is risky. You may consider sector mutual funds which are managed, but most have restrictions such as holding periods and fees. Most if not all sector mutual funds do not have contra funds that expect the sector to go down in value. Sector mutual funds cannot be shorted.

After the basics, this book provides many features to further refine your strategy such as technical Analysis. Beginners should use Strategy 1 in Book 2. After that, start with the technical indicators such as SMA-50% and RSI(14) with a handful of sector ETFs to rotate (suggested sectors are technology, bank, health care, housing, consumer and material).

In addition, some sectors are more profitable in different phases of a market cycle. We will examine several industry sectors and country sectors in more detail. China is affecting the global economies including ours. When the interest rates are low, it would affect bonds and stocks yielding high dividends. Many books ignore market timing. It turns out to be the most important technique as the last market plunges have had an average loss of 45%!

The keys to profitable sector rotation

Sector rotation could be very profitable and less risky than most of us may expect. However, it is volatile and risky if not properly implemented. There are two ways to profit from the following:

1. Buy the sector when it is trending up and sell when the sector is trending down. It is the common approach to sector rotation.
2. Buy at the bottom or close to of a sector and sell at the peak or close to. It is hard to detect the bottom/peak.

As described, using sector rotation, you never buy at the peak and sell at the bottom, as you need the price trend. Sometimes, the trend lasts for less than a month and sometimes it lasts for years.

Many investment subscriptions and free sites such as Finviz.com select favorable sectors every month. We assume the best-performing sector last month will perform better in the coming month or months. It does not always happen such as the tech sector in April, 2000 and the reversed direction of the drug sector in 2015. To protect your investments, use stops.

Alternatively, we can select them via simple charts as described in this book. Beginners should start with the Single Moving Average (SMA-20 and SMA-50 for 20 sessions and 50 sessions respectively) provided by Finviz.com without charting.

Detecting the bottom of a sector

It is not easy and no one can detect the bottom or the peak of a sector consistently but easier with trends. Enter the ETF for a specific sector or the SPY for the market in Finviz. Use a short-term SMA such as SMA-20 and SMA-50 (expressed in percent), and check these two parameters every week. If both SMA-20% and SMA-50% are positive, most likely the market or a sector is trending up.

For market timing, the SMA-350 (Single Moving Average with 350 sessions) detects the market quite accurately for the last two market plunges. I have tested out the "days" with different numbers and 350 is the best fit for the last two market plunges. In recent days, 400 could be a better choice to reduce the number of false alarms.

Besides technical indicators, there are hints that indicate a sector is close to the bottom. Using the ETF for the sector and check out the fundamental metrics similar to evaluating a stock. To illustrate, enter XLE in Yahoo!Finance or Finviz.com to get the current price and other info about this sector. Sites specializing in ETFs such as ETFdb that will give you more information about ETFs.

The intangibles for stocks and ETFs should be considered too. For example, in 2020, the potential decoupling with China would make a lot of U.S. chip companies less profitable.

Detecting the trend

Detecting the trend is easier than detecting the bottom/peak. To illustrate, bring up Finviz.com from your browser and enter XLE. For most sectors, I use the SMA-50 (single moving average for the last 50 days), which is readily available as one of the metrics. When the stock price is 3% above this SMA, it is most likely a buy. When it is 3% below this SMA, sell. It is simple, and it has been proven many times. Currently Finviz.com provides SMA-20% and SMA-50% only for short-term averages. For other durations, you can construct charts.

You can adjust the 50-day and the 3% (some use 1% or 5%) on how long your average holding period of an ETF or a stock that also depends on how often you want to trade). If your holding period is longer, use a higher number such as 90 days; use SMA-20 if it is shorter. If you want to trade more often use 2% instead of 3% (or use 5% if you want to trade less often).

Personally, I use 60 days if I use charts (from Yahoo!Finance among one of the many free sites that provide charts). One of my sector fund accounts requires 60 days for a minimum holding period without incurring a fee.

To detect a market crash and when to reenter the market, I use 350 days (some use 300 or 400 days). The 'days' are actually trade sessions.

The RSI(14) indicates whether the sector is overbought or oversold. RSI oscillates between zero and 100. Traditionally, and according to Wilder, the creator, RSI is considered overbought with a value above 70 and oversold with a value below 30 as described in the article. This indicator is available from Finviz.com.

(http://stockcharts.com/school/doku.php?id=chart_school:tec
hnical_indicators:relative_strength_index_rsi)

A simple way is to buy last month's winner(s). Ensure your ETFs
are not leveraged if you are conservative. Include contra ETFs
when the market is risky for aggressive investors. Here are the
links to the websites that keep track of top performers varying
from 1 to 3 months.

Seeking Alpha's ETF Hub.
http://seekingalpha.com/insight/etf-
hub/asset_class_performance/key_markets
Morning Star. Select the period (1 month for example).
http://news.morningstar.com/etf/Lists/ETFReturns.htm

What to buy

I prefer ETFs for specific sectors and the second choice is sector
funds (check out the holding period to exit without penalties). With
good analysts, most sector funds are better than ETFs in specific
sectors such as banking, drug companies and mining. Compare their
performances.

ETFs charge less for maintaining and they have all the advantages of
a stock. However, mutual funds select the stocks within a sector
selectively. Fidelity offers the most complete list of sector mutual
funds. Again, compare the 3- or 5-year performance between the
ETF and the fund in this same sector.

The third option is a top-down approach. First, when the market is
not plunging, select the most favorable sector and then the best
stocks within the sector. Many free sites provide a filter to find
favorable sectors.

Here is a list of sector ETFs.
(http://www.bloomberg.com/markets/etfs/)

Here is a list of commission-free ETFs from Fidelity.
(https://www.fidelity.com/etfs/ishares)

Some funds automatically switch sectors for you. From my experience so far, they have not proved to be very profitable. You should check out their past performances.

Favorable sectors according to the market cycle
Refer to the chapter on Market Timing and Spotting a Market Plunge for specific strategies. Close and/or adjust your positions when the market is plunging.

Favorable sectors according to the interest rate
It is similar to the above. Retailing, auto and housing are usually hurt by high interest rates. An improving economy would do the opposite.

Favorable sectors according to geography
It is not an easy task. China and India had their best performing years. The trade war with the U.S. may favor India as of 2020. Japan had one of the best years in 2013 during the last two decades. For foreign countries, currency fluctuation should be considered. Most emerging countries have their ups and downs. Most ETFs and sector funds in emerging countries buy larger companies that are more trustworthy as noted with their financial statements.

Global economies have never been that tightly connected. When the U.S. economy is down, China is affected and so are the resource-rich countries that China depends on.

Favorable and unfavorable events
The EU crisis has taken more than three years as of 4/2016 and the EU stocks are still close to the bottom. I prefer to buy ETFs or mutual funds which specialize in EU stocks, when the trend is up.

When the head of our Treasury says the interest will be lower, the market and the long-term bond funds will move up, and vice versa. To me, the interest rates will move up slowly from the 1/2014 bottom.

Recent favorable and unfavorable sectors
There are many sources to check which sectors performed best recently. Finviz.com is one of them. From the top menu bar, select Group, and the best and worst sectors will be displayed. Skip one

day or one week unless you have a special interest in these short durations. Select the duration depending on your purposes. Personally, I would use one month (or two) for my monthly rotation strategy assuming the momentum would pass to the next month.

Technical analysis would help to spot the trend. Select the Simple Moving Average. It is similar to the TA used in the chapter spotting a market crash. Instead of using SPY or another ETF market index, use an ETF that represents the sector.

Sector rotation by fund managers

We cannot beat these institutional investors. We need to follow them, or be one step ahead of them. They rotate sectors when they find another sector that has better appreciation potential, or the current favorable sector has reached its peak.

When to rotate

Rotate for the following reasons:
1. When the market is plunging, rotate the sector ETFs and/or mutual funds to cash. Aggressive investors would rotate their equities to contra ETFs. The average loss of the last two market plunges had been about 45%. This chart will not determine the peak (or bottom) as it depends on the falling data. However, it will tell you when to exit to prevent a further loss and tell you when to reenter the market.
2. When the fundamentals of the current sector you owned are turning bad.
3. When there is another sector that has better appreciation potential. Finviz.com tells you the rankings of the sectors.
4. When the sector is overbought or peaking, and / or has met our objective.

Do not forget about market timing

Do NOT buy any stocks except the contra ETFs for an aggressive investor, when the market is plunging. Playing defense usually wins the game more often than playing offense. When the market is peaking, protect your profits by placing stop loss orders.

Positions and how often to switch

It depends on the size of your portfolio and how much time you can afford to monitor your portfolio. To me, it varies from 2 to 6 positions and 20 to 90 days to monitor these switches.

Statistics show that a portfolio with 5 positions rotating in 20 days gives you slightly better performance and less drawback (maximum loss for the period). I recommend 4 (2 for a portfolio of less than $20,000) and 30 days (and 60 days for Fidelity sector funds). You determine according to your portfolio size and the time available to you for investing.

Conclusion

Sector rotation is described in very basic terms here. The links in Afterthoughts provide additional information.

As a reminder, **roughly half of a stock's price movement can be attributed to the sector** it is in.

Afterthoughts

- There are many articles on this topic. They are:
  Sector rotation strategies ETF investors must know. There are many useful links.
  http://www.bloomberg.com/markets/etfs/

  Sector rotation based on performance.
  http://stockcharts.com/school/doku.php?id=chart_school:tradi ng_strategies:sector_rotation roc
  Fidelity on Sectors.
  https://www.fidelity.com/sector-investing/overview
  Video instruction.
  http://www.YouTube.com/watch?v=j5yYoOoATRM
- No one can consistently predict the bottom or the peak of any sector. Sometimes we move in too early and lose another 25% or so, or we leave the sector too early to lose another 25% or so potential gain. It is quite normal. Learn why we move within the wrong time frame, and a lot of times it may be just bad luck or other events that are beyond our control.
- A free (as of this writing) service on sector rotation.
  http://www.gosector.com/

More links from YouTube

Simple sector rotation, 2, another 3

https://www.youtube.com/watch?v=FOKTFFabpL8
https://www.youtube.com/watch?v=85IRL_3oR8&t=219s
https://www.youtube.com/watch?v=gu-46zcBwsI&t=177s
https://www.youtube.com/watch?v=MFVmEcRHpnk

#Filler: My daughter's wedding banquet

How do you have a wedding banquet that the entire town will talk about and at the least cost? It is at the Burger King where they treat you like a king. All the fries are super-sized and the drinks are bottomless. The king's crown and the most popular party favor, are included. Of course, my daughter flatly refused.

2   Outline on how to start sector rotation

As with everything in life, there is no guarantee that this book will make you a lot of money. However, the chance of success will be substantially improved especially when you practice with most of the ideas presented in this book. Always start with paper trading first.

1. First determine your objectives. Retirees select safer strategies. Millionaires can afford to select riskier strategies for larger returns.

2. Determine your risk tolerance, how much time you have for investing, your knowledge of investing, and your desire to continue to learn about investing and your portfolio size.

   To illustrate, when the market is risky, do not buy any stock. However, for investors who can tolerate higher risk, buy contra ETFs as a hedge against the market for larger returns. Retirees may be less risk tolerant unless they're rich.

   If your job is very demanding, you should spend less time in investing even if you're knowledgeable on investing and have a desire to learn about investing.

   Check your net worth (= what you own – what you owe) and cash flow (incomes – debt payments). Reserve your emergency cash equal to your expenses for at least 3 months.

   If the above is limited, SPY or any ETF simulating the market is your only sector and market timing is your primary tool (Book 2, Strategy 1, Chapter 2). You can stop here for now, and continue reading the rest of the book when the limitations change.

3. When the market is peaking, invest cautiously. Use trailing stops described in this book. The same for your sector ETFs / funds that have appreciated a lot.

4. When you have lost two trades in a row, take a break and return to paper trading until you're comfortable.

5. Test your strategies on paper. This book requires you to try out the various strategies, and select the one you are comfortable with. All theories may not always work for real trading.

6. When a strategy has been thoroughly tested out recently and the results are good, use real money slowly and gradually. Then monitor your performance.

7. When you have a new strategy or you need to test a strategy whether it works in the current market, read "Testing strategies".

Not all of the predictions (mine or others) have materialized, and no strategy is evergreen. Always use stops to protect your portfolio. Learn from your arguments for the predictions, not merely the accuracy of the predictions. Predictions are based on educated guesses, and hence hopefully more of them will materialize in the long run. Consult your financial advisor before investing with real money.

The rest of this book describes the other aspects of sector rotation such as Top-Down Investing (in case you prefer to find the stocks in the favorable sector), country sectors, specific industry sectors… Many investing ideas described here are applicable to other investing strategies.

#Filler: lessons from a strategy named Turtle with my inputs

The experiment to train students who have no experience in two weeks worked. The technical analysis strategy would not work today for many reasons. However, the concepts are still good and explained here.

Do not time the market (not agree totally). Find a good strategy (easier said than done) and stick with it consistently. Cash management (agree with stops from 5% to 15% depending on your risk tolerance and the volatility of the stocks). Do not use leverage that could wipe out your entire portfolio. Follow the trend of the stock with higher positions.

3 Sectors

The primary sectors are: Materials, Consumer Discretionary, Consumer Staples, Energy, Financial, Real Estate, Health Care, Industrial, Information Technology and Utilities. Click the above links from Fidelity, or search from Fidelity, Investopedia and/or Wikipedia for a description of these sectors.

We can subdivide a sector into sub sectors (a.k.a. industries). For example, Information Technology can be divided into Computer and Software. When the computer industry is good, it does not mean that the software industry is also good. Some industries such as banking software can belong to more than one sector (banking and software in this example).

Fidelity has its own definition and overview as described in this link: https://www.fidelity.com/sector-investing/overview

In the above links, Fidelity describes sectors pretty well. Many vendors including IBD provide industry rankings. You may want to select the best sector or industry first and then select the best stocks in that sector or industry.

GIGS (developed by MSCI and S&P 500) separates more than 29,000 stocks into 11 major sectors: consumer discretionary, consumer staples, energy, financials, industrials, information technology, materials, telecommunication services, utilities and health care. It is very similar to Fidelity but GIGS's industry classification is more complicated to deploy. Most other sources do not follow GIGS's industry classification. Here is my additional description to cover the basic sectors and some will be described in more detail in their appropriate strategies that follow.

Materials
Material should be separated into two categories: Basic (a.k.a. Industrial) Materials and Precious Metals. Basic materials such as copper and iron rise in prices when the economy is humming, and vice versa. Precious Metals such as gold and silver do not usually correlate with basic materials. Gold and silver usually rise due to high inflation, political unrest and/or falling USD.

Consumer Staples and Discretionary

Consumer Staples are food, beverages, household products and the products we buy as necessities. They are recession-proof. Our products have demonstrated high quality and safety. With the growing middle class in developing countries such as China and India, we expect they should grow well outside the USA. In early 2020, it was not the case due to the trade war. Consumer Discretionary are just the opposite. For example, car sales would be down in a recession.

Energy

Energy has many sub sectors (a.k.a. industries) such as clean energy, exploring, distribution, refining and even all of the above (using the term 'integrate'). When the economy is growing, usually energy sectors rise in price. When the market and/or oil price falls, Saudi Arabia, the largest oil exporter, would dump more oil and hence it would make the oil price fall further.

Financial

The sub sectors are banks, mortgage companies, brokerages (a tough industry with no commission trades today), insurance companies and many other financial institutions. This sector would plunge during a recession. In the period of 2007 and 2008, this sector had a tough time.

Real Estate

Besides housing construction, this sector is primarily made up of companies that own and/or build properties and REITs. This sector should not do well during a recession.

Health Care

It should be divided into many sub sectors: hospitals, research / development of medical equipment and drugs. In some sense, hospitals and generic drugs also belong to Consumer Staples that you need to use or buy regardless of the condition of the economy. Most likely, we do not need new equipment and new drugs in a depressed economy.

Industrial

This sector includes Boeing, construction equipment companies such as Caterpillar and defense companies. Most of GE's subsidiaries belong to this sector. With the global economies slowing down and the problems with Boeing in 2019, this sector has not been doing well in 2020.

Information technology

It is a very wide sector covering hardware companies and software companies. If Telecommunication is not a separate sector, it should be under this sector too. Microsoft, Facebook and Apple are under this sector. From 1/2010 to 1/2020, this sector is very profitable. With the decoupling with China, the profits will be reduced.

Utilities

It is a consumer staple sector. However, we use more electricity, fuels and water when the economy is humming.

Other sectors

Transportation, Services and Retail should be separate sectors but are not classified so by many institutions. Retail has had a tough time since the rise of Amazon, and now it is even worse during the pandemic of 2020.

Links

A list of sectors.
http://www.investorguide.com/sector-list.php
Check's sector analysis.
http://seekingalpha.com/article/2806655-the-stock-market-2015-a-sector-by-sector-valuation-perspective-part-1-an-overview

#Filler: My grandson

My six-year-old grandson called the library about the availability of the book Mine Craft. The lady told him that only "Mine Craft for Dummies" was available. He told her it was not for him as he was not a dummy.

4   Subsectors (i.e., Industries) and sector funds

Sectors are further divided into subsectors (same as <u>industries</u>). For example, Oil Energy is a sector while Oil Exploration and Oil Service are industries. Industries cover a very specialized segment of the sector, so they consist of fewer companies and sometimes smaller companies; they are more volatile and hence riskier. To illustrate, the ETF for an industry (say Oil Exploration) has less companies than the entire sector Oil Energy. Some industry ETFs such as Uranium are very small with a handful of stocks; they are highly volatile with high risk.

Sector mutual funds are managed by fund managers who select stocks instead of including most stocks in the sector. The disadvantages over ETFs are fees, restrictions of holding periods (the usual 1 to 2 months) without a penalty, offering fewer industries and you cannot short a fund.

SeekingAlpha.com has a good performance summary for each sector including many countries and industries. Select the best ETF from the last month, use stop loss to protect momentum reversal and switch when there is a better sector or industry to buy. Aggressive investors can also short an ETF, or buy contra ETFs for the worst performed sectors or industries.

Filler

I got a call from Buffett asking me to lead their stock research.
I asked him why for nobody such as myself. No kidding.

He told me that he should have read my book Scoring Stocks to buy Apple instead of IBM in May, 2013. It would save his company millions of dollars minus $10 for my book. Not to mention the market timing technique that had worked in the last two major market plunges.

I told him, "OK, I'll beat your mediocre returns of the last 5 years."
He said, "You can do better than that and at least beat SPY. If you do so, no one will be that stupid to leave my fund and pay the hefty capital gain taxes."

I told him, "I cannot beat the market as you are the market especially after your expensive fees. In addition, I do not know how to avoid day traders from riding my wagon in trading. Also, most of my big profits were made in small stocks that your fund cannot trade besides owning the company."

I woke up trembling. I'm glad it is only a nightmare.

5 Selecting ETFs

Judging by the popularity, ETFs are a better way to rotate within sectors compared to sector mutual funds. Select ETFs from my ETF tables (Book 2, Strategy 3, Chapter 1). You rotate an ETF(s) from your selection of ETFs. I will explain my selection here starting from a few to about 25. It is less time-consuming to limit your selection to 4 to analyze and keep track of their performances. A larger selection gives you more choices and hence supposedly improves your performance.

The selected ETFs must have assets over 100 million. If there are two similar ETFs, check out their expense ratios. As of today, Fidelity offers commission-free for most ETFs. Check your broker for similar offerings. The corresponding sector fund is also provided in my tables; you cannot rotate ETFs with Fidelity's Annuities.

Beginners should skip subsectors (a.k.a. industries), which are riskier as they are too specialized. Skip the leveraged ETFs unless you can bear the risk.

Some sectors, especially the subsectors, are more volatile than others and they would be on the top and bottom performers more frequently. From Finviz.com or other sources, check out the RSI(14) to ensure the sector is not overbought (i.e., the value is greater than 65). I prefer to select the one of the top ETFs with a lower volatility and an RSI(14) between 30 and 60. From my testing using ETFReplay, it is better to use 2 months rather than 20 trade days for selecting the best-performing ETFs.

Starting with ETFs

To start, I recommend the following ETFs: SPY and GLD (in the risky 2020). Add a money market fund, or a bond ETF with a short duration when the market is risky. Beginners should NOT use SH (a contra ETF to SPY) for monthly rotation and only aggressive investors should buy SH when the market is plunging.

Add the following ETFs to broaden your selection on market cap: DIA, QQQ, SPYG, SPYV, NOBL, IWM, IWC and BOND. The market may favor very large companies (DOW), tech (QQQ), growth (SPYG), value (SPYV), NOBL (dividend), mid cap (MDY), small cap (IWM) and microcap (IWC; risky). Add a total bond (BOND) if desirable. Optionally I add buy back (PKW) and momentum (MTUM).

It is better not to include bond funds in monthly rotation. Long term bond funds rise opposite of the interest rate.

Skip foreign countries if you do not want to take the foreign exchange risk. Otherwise, I would include some foreign exposure: small cap (SCZ), Europe (VGK), China (FXI), Latin America (ILF), EFA(EAFE), global (KXI) and VWO (Emerging; risky).

If you're into specific foreign countries, add Australia (EWA), Brazil (EWZ), Canada (EWC), India (INDY), Indonesia (EIDO), Hong Kong (EWH), Japan (EWJ), Singapore (EWS), Taiwan (EWT), United Kingdom (EWU) and Vietnam (VNM; profitable if decoupling with China).

The last selection could be the only selection for some investors specialized in industry sectors (a.k.a. sub sectors). They are the industry sectors: bank (KBE), Bio (XBI), consumer discretionary (XLY), consumer staple (XLP), finance (IYF), energy (XLE), health care (IYH), house builders (ITB), industrial (IYJ), material (XME), oil (USO), oil service (OIH), oil exploration (XOP), gas (UNG), real estate (VNQ), retail (RTH), regional banking (KRE), semiconductor (SMH), software (XSW) and technology (XLK).

My summaries from testing (mainly from using ETFReplay):
- Slightly better results using relative strength of 1 month than 2 months.
  1 month means 20 trade sessions (30 days - 10 weekends / holidays).
  Relative strength means picking the best performing ETF from your selected group of ETFs.

- There were better results not using contra ETFs (could be due to our long bull market from 2009), so I skipped them especially for beginners.
- The same for interest-sensitive ETFs, so I actually skipped them.
- Do not include the offending sectors that caused the market to crash – these sectors take longer to recover. They were the technology in 2000 and the banks / house construction in 2008.

#Filler: Ambition is good

That is what I heard from the web. The little girl wanted to be a president when she grew up. After attending a circus, she wanted to be a clown. Her smart father told her that she could be both. When a kid wants to be a president, most likely the kid will be a good citizen.

Filler

I got a call from Buffett asking me to lead their stock research.
I asked him why for nobody such as myself. No kidding.

He told me that he should have read my book Scoring Stocks to buy Apple instead of IBM in May, 2013. It would save his company millions of dollars minus $10 for my book. Not to mention the market timing technique that had worked in the last two major market plunges.

I told him, "OK, I'll beat your mediocre returns of the last 5 years."
He said, "You can do better than that and at least beat SPY. If you do so, no one will be that stupid to leave my fund and pay the hefty capital gain taxes."

I told him, "I cannot beat the market as you are the market especially after your expensive fees. In addition, I do not know how to avoid day traders from riding my wagon in trading. Also, most of my big profits were made in small stocks that your fund cannot trade besides owning the company."

I woke up trembling. I'm glad it is only a nightmare.

#Filler: Miss Mia

In my first job and just after the Vietnam War, everyone (yes, guys and ladies) tried to date my beautiful officemate Mia except me. If we married, then her name would be Mia Pow ('missing-in-action' and 'prisoner-of-war'). She would be very popular or very unpopular without showing her beautiful face. In any case, when she becomes a mother, she will be Mamma Mia.

The common ETFs for indexes

There are three ETFs for each of the indexes: DOW, S&P 500 and NASDAQ.

DOW has only 30 large stocks. The ETF is DIA. It is not diversified for me, so I skip it most of the time.

S&P 500 index represents the market to most with about 500 large companies. One of the common ETFs is SPY.

NASDAQ index represents about 3,000 large companies and many of them are technology companies. QQQ has about 100 large companies from this index.

Both DIS, SPY and QQQ are market-cap weighed. From 1/2020 to 7/2020, QQQ is doing the best as many of the top holdings are breaking records.

When the market goes down, the biggest winner may turn into the biggest loser. To reduce potential losses, you may want to select ETFs, not market-cap weighed. They are EDOW, RSP and QQQE for DIA, SPY and QQQ respectively.

The following ETFs VTI, MDY, IWM and IWC represent Total Market, Mid Cap, Small Cap and Micro Cap respectively.

Currently, you cannot short stocks in retirement accounts, but you can buy contra ETFs in any account.

6 How to find the current best-performing sectors

There are many websites that will show you the current best-performing sectors or ETFs for sectors. Depending on the website, some may give you the best-performed ETFs for the last month or the last 30 days for example. If you rotate among a few sectors, you can maintain a record of their performance.

Seeking Alpha's home page has further divided the ETFs into the following groups: Sector, Industry (sub sector) and country. Pick the site you use most and/or your broker's site for this information.

Fidelity

Click on "News & Research" and then "Stock Market & Sector Performance" for sector performance and weighing recommendations. Fidelity offers the most choices for sector funds plus many sector commission-free ETFs. Most sector funds have penalties if you hold them less than 30 days (60 days for most sector funds in an annuity). Check the current restrictions.

7 How to determine a reversal

This article describes two basic ways to detect a reversal of trend. For illustration purposes, I describe the reversal of an uptrend. The reversal of a downtrend follows similar logic. Volume is the confirmation. Detecting reversal is a technique and it does not always work. Hence, use stops to protect your portfolio and review the stops every week or two for rising stocks.

Simple method

When the SMA-20 (from Finviz.com) drops below SMA-50, it is an indication that the uptrend could be over. For a longer holding period, it is the SMA-50 dropping below SMA-200. If both SMA-20 and SMA-50 are negative, most likely the uptrend turns to a downtrend. You can confirm it with volume; a low volume is not a confirmation.

If it is vastly overbought (RSI(14) > 65) and the volume is low, it could mean that there are no buyers for the ETF. If the peak has occurred, do not be the last one holding that ETF.

ETFs and stocks are normally traded in a range between the resistance and the support. However, when the trend is up and the volume is high, the chance of breaking up the resistance is high. The opposite applies: When the trend is down and the volume is high, the chance of breaking up the support is high.

Complicated method

Method 1. Head and Shoulder is a reliable chart pattern to predict a trend reversal. Basically, the uptrend is running out of momentum and hence the reversal (i.e., downturn) is possible. The head indicates a price peak and followed by a smaller peak.

Method 2. A Candlestick chart tells more about an ETF's or stock's movement. Basically, it shows the opening price, the closing price and the price fluctuations for the day (or the week if selected). The white body means it is an up day while the black body indicates a down day.

When the candlestick is black (meaning a down day) and is larger than the previous day which is white, it could indicate the uptrend is reversing. The technical term is engulfed candlestick.

When the candlestick returns back to an uptrend, it means the trend is still up and the engulfed candlestick on the second day is a false indicator. It involves 3 candlesticks. It is a more complicated topic.

Link: Reversal: https://www.youtube.com/watch?v=uO4yJGSz1vU

Sector rotation Profit by being early.
https://www.youtube.com/watch?v=MFVmEcRHpnk

https://www.youtube.com/watch?v=evgsloYNsek

8   SMA, MACD and Volume

Bring up Finviz.com. Enter SPY for your ticket symbol. The market trend is up if both SMA-20 and SMA-50 are positive. Finviz.com uses percent to indicate how far away the current price is above the average. The daily change of volume is also displayed. It is the confirmation indicator. When the price rises with low volume, it may not indicate the trend is up.

Use MACD for better results. For simplicity, the trend is up when MACD is above the 0 line (usually in green color), and vice versa.

Most use daily charts (charting is not for beginners). Weekly charts should be used if the duration of holding the stock is longer. The above also applies for stocks trending down.

Filler: Happy Mother's Day Poem
(This is my translation from a Chinese poet Yee. I made some changes due to the loss in translation.)

I cried at two unforgettable times in my life.

The first time I came to this world.
The second time you left this world.

The first time I did not know but from your mouth.
The second time you did not know but from my heart.

Between these two crises, we had endless laughs.
For the last 30 years, we had joyful laughs that had been repeated, repeated...

You treasured every laugh.
I cherish every laugh for the rest of my life.

9   Evaluating a sector

"Section I and Chapter 6" describes how to find the current-performing sectors via free websites such as Seeking Alpha and Fidelity (requiring opening an account). This article describes how you can do it yourself.

The following is for illustration only. The figures are from 12/20/2020 and the sector is "XLK", the technology sector.

Determining the trend

Bring up Finviz.com from your browser. Enter "XLK" for the ticker (stock symbol).

From the graph, it shows it is in an uptrend.

Most of us use SMA50 (Simple Moving Average for the last 50 sessions). It is 6%, and hence the ETF is up. SMA20 is for the average holding period of the last 20 sessions, and is 3%. The percentage gives us how the average is above the current price.

My holding period is about 30 sessions and I use the average value. In this case it is about 4.5%. If you want to be more precise, you can open a chart and specify 30 sessions for SMA.

SMA200 is for long-term hold, and most of us do not care about it for short-term sector rotation.

Other parameters

RSI(14). If it is higher than 65, watch out for oversold conditions, which could indicate a higher chance to reverse the trend. Some sectors just keep on rising. The best way is to use trailing stops (you update the stops every week or so from the current prices).

P/E. It is not available on Finviz.com. Bring up ETFdb.com. From the Search icon, enter XLK. It indicates a P/E of 28.57. It is a better value than the average of most sectors; it ranks 18 out of 42. For Sector Rotation, value parameters such as P/E are not that important as the trend value.

Holdings. Click on Holdings in ETFdb. This ETF is weighed by Market Cap and Apple comprises of about 24% of the Assets. The next one is Microsoft with 19% of the Assets. It is quite risky, and not as diversified as expected. These two stocks are about 43% of the total Assets of this ETF. If you have $100,000 to invest, you can invest 24% of the $100,000 in Apple and 19% of $100,000 in Microsoft. In this way, you have better control and save the management fees.

Many parameters such as Finviz's Debt/Equity, Insiders' Transactions, Short%, Quarter-to-Quarter Sales and Profits can be estimated by making the proportional averages of these parameters of these two stocks.

Other parameters from ETFdb
Technical.

SMAs are available here. I prefer the percentages from Finviz.

Beta of 1.06 in this example indicates this ETF is more volatile than the average stock. MACD, Bollinger Brands, Supports / Resistance and Stochastic are available. They are useful, but you have to fully understand these technical parameters.

Intangibles

There are other considerations that affect the performance of the sector. Apple could be a victim of the trade war with China. There are many sectors that will be affected by today's pandemic. For example, in Feb, 2020, we should know the pandemic was coming. At that time, you should unload the affected ETFs and those stocks related to travel such as airlines and cruise lines if you had them. The riskier investors should consider shorting them. The excessive printing of money would give rise to ETFs related to commodities.

One strategy

Find the best sectors with best values (based on P/E for example) and select the top one or two best momentum ETFs as described here.
https://www.youtube.com/watch?v=uwfrdxxtULk

10   A simple but risky strategy on market timing

Follow the article "Simplest Market Timing" to time the market. If it tells you the market is going down, buy contra ETFs and/or move stocks to cash depending on your risk tolerance.

Recommended ETFs (5 total)
SPY
PSQ
SEF
GLD
Money Market / CD

My reasons
Contra ETFs are betting the sectors represented to go down. During a market downturn, I would bet against bank/financial stocks (SEF, a contra ETF for the financial sector) and tech stocks (PSQ, a contra ETF for NASDAQ which includes a lot of tech stocks).

GLD is an ETF for gold. During a recession, gold should fare better than stocks, but it may not perform most of the contra ETFs. If the value of the USD depreciates, gold would fare better. Every portfolio should have 2 to 10% in gold depending on your risk tolerance. If you are conservative, move everything to Money Market fund / CD instead of the contra ETFs when the market is crashing.

We have only one false alarm from 2000 to 2010 but more after 2010. The false alarm tells you to exit the market and then tells you to reenter the market shortly. If you do not buy any contra ETFs, most likely you do not lose much.

After the crash
When the market timing tells you to return to the market, sell contra ETFs and buy SPY (or any ETF that simulates the market) and value stocks. You need more time to find and evaluate value stocks, so buy SPY or similar ETFs first. Use stops to protect your portfolio, as we never know whether it is a false recovery or not.

11 Money Market, CDs & Bonds

Overview

CDs are suitable for conservative investors or for temporarily parking money during market downturns. While they offer lower returns compared to stocks or ETFs, they provide stability in uncertain times.

Key Points about CDs

1. Rates and Returns:
   - One-year CD rates have varied from 1.5% in 2020 to 4% in 2024.
   - After accounting for inflation and taxes, returns may be negative. CDs serve better as a defensive investment rather than for growth.
2. Laddering Strategy:
   To ensure liquidity while maximizing returns:
   - Split your investment across CDs with staggered maturity dates (e.g., 3 months, 12 months).
   - Renew maturing CDs for shorter terms to adjust for changing interest rates.
3. FDIC Insurance:
   - FDIC insures up to $250,000 per bank, not per account.
   - Some foreign bank CDs are also FDIC-insured and may offer higher rates.
4. Tax Considerations:
   - CDs from local banks may receive favorable tax treatment in some states.
   - However, brokered CDs often offer better rates and convenience.
5. Avoid Callable CDs:
   - Callable CDs allow banks to terminate the agreement early, typically when rates drop.
   - Be careful on non-callable CDs unless the offered rates are significantly higher.

Alternatives to CDs

- Money Market Funds:
  Brokers like Fidelity offer competitive money market funds (e.g., SPAXX). These provide liquidity and variable yields but are more sensitive to interest rate changes.
- Bond Funds and ETFs:
  Bond funds like HYG or JNK provide higher yields but come with added risk. Remember, bond prices generally fall when interest rates rise. The following is my illustration.

Their annualized returns are compounded. SPY is the benchmark I use. Check out their past performances. In 2008, the market crashed. It was a bad year for both bond funds and ETFs, but the bond funds lose less than SPY.

	2007	2008	2009
HYG	3%	-18%	29%
JNK	Not avail.	-25%	38%
SPY	5%	-37%	26%

Link: Government bond default?
https://www.youtube.com/watch?v=wMxj6iB92ZA
- Broker CDs (Recommended):
  https://www.youtube.com/watch?v=zhEiyW2N7KE
- More on CD: https://www.youtube.com/watch?v=FRWMsGJ2-NE
- Money market fund:
  https://www.youtube.com/watch?v=N53wZ_80abU
- Its risk: https://www.youtube.com/watch?v=k3wGqD_9SzY
- Better than cash:
  https://www.youtube.com/watch?v=SrQTOhafE4A

12 Anatomy of a trade

- Ensure the market is trending up before you trade (Chapter 7). You do not need charting knowledge. It is simpler than it looks.

- Beginners. If you are not ready to buy stocks, buy CDs with different maturing dates (Chapter 1). Buy ETF(s) such as VOO, a low-fee ETF for S&P 500 index.

- Non-beginners. Screen stocks with the screens that have the best performances recently. Evaluate stocks with metrics from Finviz.com such as avoiding stocks being dumped by the insiders, negative Q-Q earnings, etc.

- Metrics are generally divided into short term and long term. For me, long term means holding the acquired stocks for more than one year.

- Consider the lower taxes on capital gains on non-retirement accounts.

- Recommend buying less than 10 stocks with less than 3 stocks in the same sector. To illustrate, for a $10,000 portfolio, buy 10 stocks with a position of $1,000 each.

- Sell stocks when your objectives are met or the market is trending down (Chapter 7).

- The reason why investors making good profits when their success rates are only 50%: stop orders. Many recommend set stops so you can lose only 5% (or 10% for volatile stocks) of a trade. Use trailing stops for winners (i.e. periodically renew the stop based on the current price).

Everyone's situation is different, so tailor the above to your own requirements, knowledge and available time for investing. Usually, I hold more than 10 stocks and I use covered calls to maximize my profits.

Do not put new money on losers but on gainers if the trend is positive. The above are my opinions only. Read the Disclaimer in the Introduction section.

Section II: Strategies:

Strategy 1: Market Timing

1   The power of market timing

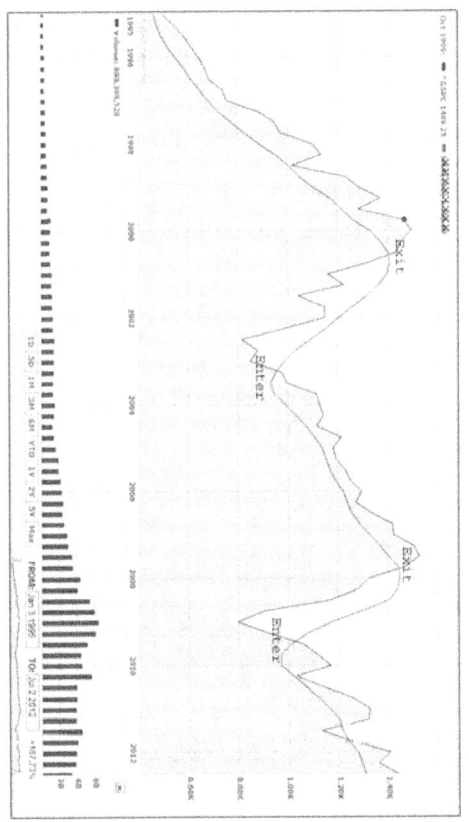

Most e-book readers allow you to select the graph to make it fit entirely on your screen. I use SPY, an ETF simulating the market. Detecting market plunges as seen in this graph indicates the exit points and reentry points also from 2000 to 9-2009 as follows.

Market Plunge	Peak	Bottom	Indicator Exit	Indicator Reenter
2000	08/28/00	09/20/02	10/01/00	06/01/03
2007	10/12/07	03/06/09	02/01/08	09/01/09
			08/01/11	11/01/11

Table: Vital Dates

For simplicity I skipped a few brief exits and reentries since 2011. You can run the simple chart once a month. When it indicates a potential market plunge is close, run the chart once a week. The last row   represents   a   false   signal.

This is based on stock prices so it may not identify the peaks and bottoms precisely, but so far it has not failed to avoid big losses and ensure big gains by reentering the market. I hope the next market plunge would give us enough time to act as these two did.

Unbelievable return with market timing
Calculate how much you made if you followed the above exit points and reenter points from 2000 to today. I bet you would have made a good fortune. I compared the above returns with the SPY without market timing from 1-2000 to 9-2013.

There are many assumptions. Dividends and compounding are not considered. My return should be substantially better if I include buying contra ETFs during the exits and selling them during the reentries. I was shocked by the incredible return by using this simple market timing. Again, past performance does not guarantee future performances.

Summary info:

S&P 500 1-2000 to 9-2013	With Market Timing	Without Market Timing
Better	**500%**	
Gain	1,000	167
Gain %	68%	11%
Annualized gained	5%	1%
Days	4,959	4,959

Calculations:

S & P 500	With Market Timing	Without Market Timing
1-2000	1,469[1]	1,469[1]
Exit 10/01/00	1,041[2]	1,041
Enter 06/01/03	1,041	964[4]
Exit 02/01/08	1,489[3]	1,379[4]
Enter 09/01/09	1489	1,020[5]
Exit 08/01/11	1,888	1,293
Enter 11/01/11	1,888	1,251
09/03/13	2,469	1.638
Gained	2,469 – 1,469=1,000	1,638-1,469=167
Gain %	1000/1469 = 68%	167/1469 = 11%
Annualized %	68% * 365/4959=5%	11%*365/4959=1%

Better	(1,000-167)/167 = 500%	

Portfolio with Market Timing:

[1] Both start with S&P 500 of 1,469 on 1-3-2000.
[2] 10/01/00
The market timing portfolio exits the market and remains the same value of 1,041 until 6/1/00.
[3]   02/01/08
The market timing portfolio exits the market and remains the same value of 1,489 until 9/1/09.

'1,489' is calculated as follows:
$1,041 * (1 + Rate) = 1,041 * (1 + 1,379-964)/964) = 1,489$
where the S&P 500 is 964 on 6/1/00 and 1,379 on 2/1/08.

The other calculations are based on the S&P 500 at 1,020 on 9/1/9, 1,293 on 8/1/11, 1,251 on 11/1/11 and 1,636 on 9/3/13.

Portfolio without Market Timing:

[1] Both starts with the S&P 500 of 1,469 on 1-3-2000. We could use the 9/3/13 the S&P 500 value, but it would not account for some compounded interest considerations.

[4] S&P 500 is 964 on 6/1/00 and 1,379 on 2/1/08.

[5] 02/01/08. The portfolio value is calculated to be 1,020 as follows:
$1,379 * (1 + Rate) = 1,379 * (1 + (1020-1379)/1379) = 1,020$
where S&P 500 is 1,379 on 2/1/08 and 1,020 on 9/1/09.

The other calculations are based on the S&P 500 at 1,293 on 8/1/11, 1,251 on 11/1/11 and 1,636 on 9/3/13.

I cannot believe the shocking return with market timing. I checked my calculations and there was nothing wrong that I could find. If you find something wrong, send your findings to me (pow_tony@yahoo.com). Even if I made a mistake somehow and got 100% instead of 500%, it still doubles the return without market timing! Ask any fund manager what it means to his or her fund performance and his / her career.

2   Simplest market timing

Why Market Timing Matters

Before the 2000s, market timing was often dismissed. However, with major market plunges (e.g., 2000 and 2008) averaging losses of 45%, timing has become a practical tool to minimize losses and improve overall returns.

The goal of market timing is not to predict exact peaks and bottoms but to reduce exposure during downturns and re-enter during recoveries. Using Finviz, no charting is used.

Most gurus do not believe in market timing. The following simple techniques have been proven profitable in 2000 and 2008 market plunges. Accumulate cash when the market plunges and re-enter the market when the indicator tells you so. My most profitable years are the early recovery stage of the market for both 2000 and 2008.

My key Indicators for Market Timing

1. **Death Cross:**
   o   Occurs when the 50-day Simple Moving Average (SMA-50) crosses below the 200-day Simple Moving Average (SMA-200. Note: I use 200 as it is readily available from Finviz).
   o   Signals a potential market plunge.
2. **Golden Cross:**
   o   Occurs when SMA-50 crosses above SMA-200.
   o   Indicates market recovery and signals it's time to re-enter.

How to Detect a Market Plunge

- **Use a site like Finviz:**
   1. Search for SPY or RSP (representing the S&P 500). Check the SMA metrics:
      - SMA-200%: Positive values suggest no immediate downturn.

- SMA-50% vs. SMA-200%: If SMA-50 is more negative than SMA-200, it signals a market plunge.
2. Look for a negative trend in the Buy/Sell ratio (B/S) week over week.

Action Steps During a Plunge:

- **Conservative Approach:**
  o Sell riskier stocks (e.g., those with negative earnings or high P/E ratios).
  o Hold cash or low-risk assets like CDs or money market funds.
- **Aggressive Approach:**
  o Sell all stocks.
  o Consider buying contra ETFs like PSQ (shorts the NASDAQ) or SH (shorts the S&P 500).

How to Detect Market Recovery

- **Reverse the process used for detecting a plunge:**
  1. SMA-200% turns positive.
  2. SMA-50% crosses above SMA-200% (Golden Cross).
  3. Look for a positive week-over-week trend in the Buy/Sell ratio.

Action Steps During Recovery:

- Sell contra ETFs and close short positions.
- Reinvest cash in broad-market ETFs like SPY or VOO.

Tips for Monitoring Indicators

- Frequency: Check indicators monthly. Increase to weekly if prices approach SMA thresholds.
- Advanced Method: For fewer false signals, use SMA-350 (or SMA-400) instead of SMA-200.

Limitations of Market Timing

- Does not capture exact market peaks or bottoms due to reliance on past data.
- False signals may lead to minor losses (e.g., selling early and re-entering).
- Requires discipline to follow the strategy despite market noise or volatility.

Example Application

As of February 12, 2022:

ETF	SMA-200%	SMA-50%	Death Cross?
SPY	-0.8%	-4.2%	Yes
RSP	-0.5%	-1.9%	Yes

This data indicated a confirmed market downturn, suggesting a shift to defensive assets.

Another Simple chart example.

Bring up StockCharts.com and enter SPY. It indicates Death Cross occurred on around March 20, 2022.

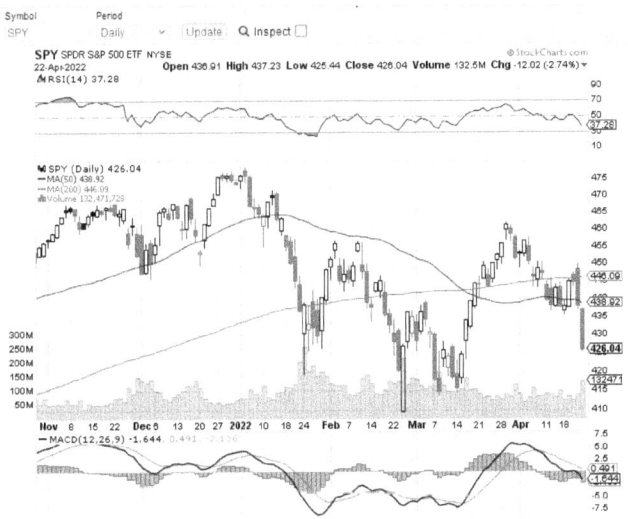

Strategy 2: Rotation of 4 Sectors

Rotate sectors via ETFs and/or mutual funds. When the market is risky, move them to cash, short-term bond ETF/mutual fund, money market fund or a combination of the above and reenter when the market is not risky.

1   Rotate four ETFs

We can beat the market by rotating one ETF that represents the market such as SPY and cash via market timing. Aggressive investors can add SH or PSQ (contra ETFs) to the four to have better returns during market plunges.

During a market uptrend, rotating the following four ETFs could be more profitable than staying with SPY (or any ETF that simulates the market). Be warned that a short-term capital gain in taxable accounts is not treated as favorably as the long-term capital gain; check current tax laws.

The allocation percentages depend on your individual risk tolerance. You can use indexed mutual funds. Compare their expenses and restrictions. Some mutual funds charge you if you withdraw within a specific time period.

Select the best performer of last month (from Seeking Alpha, cnnFn, or one of many ETF/mutual fund sites). Add a contra ETF such as SH to take advantage of a falling market for more aggressive investors. Add sector ETFs to the described four ETFs such as XLY, XLP, XLE, XLF, XLU, IYW, XHB, IYM, OIL and XLU to expand your selection.

ETFs	Money Market	U.S.	International	Bond
Fidelity		Spartan Total Market	Spartan Global Market	Spartan US Bond
Vanguard		Total Stock Market	Total International Market	Total Bond Market
My choice	Fidelity	SPY	Vanguard	Fidelity
Suggest %				

During Market plunge	90%	0%	0%	10%
After plunge	10%	60%	20%	10%

Explanation

- The above are suggestions only. If your broker offers similar ETFs, consider using them.
- Check out any restrictions of the ETFs and commissions.
- 4 ETFs (one actually is a money market fund) are enough for most starters. They are diversified, low-cost and you do not need rebalancing except during a market plunge.
- The percentages are suggestions only. If you are less risk tolerant, allocate more to a money market fund, CD and/or bond ETF.
- Have at least 10% allocated to the money market fund for safety.
- When the market is risky, reduce stock equities (i.e., increase money market and bond allocations).
- The symbols for Fidelity ETFs are FSTMX, FSGDX and FBIDX.
- The symbols for Vanguard ETFs are VTSMX, VGTSX and VBMFX.
- If you are more advanced, use additional sector ETFs to rotate. Also buy long-term bond funds (such as 30-year Treasury) when the interest rate is 10% or more.

#Filler: Glad to be an investor

After watching the following YouTube video, I am glad my parents did not push me to play piano and also glad I do not have any musical gene. How can I compete with this kid?

https://www.youtube.com/watch?v=yf0B4rVoq44

Also, glad not into some life-threatening professions such as surgical doctors, soldiers, fire fighters, etc. I can make mistakes in investing from time to time without suffering from the consequences. With the uptrend market for most of the last 50 years, most investors should make good money. Thank God.

Strategy 3: Rotation of more sectors

It is similar to the Strategy 2 but includes more basic sectors. Add a contra ETF such as SH to take advantage of a falling market. Add the following sector ETFs to the four sectors described in Strategy 2: XLY, XLP, XLE, XLF, XLU, IYW, XHB, IYM, OIL and XLU. They should cover most of the sectors.

Start keeping the top two sectors to start. The allocation percentages depend on individual risk tolerance. You can use indexed mutual funds. Compare their expenses and restrictions.

Select the best performer of last month. Besides cnnfn.com and finviz.com, the current, favorable sectors can be found in many websites including SeekingAlpha.com and Fidelity.com (customers only). Following the top performer(s) for the last month is following the short-term trend. In addition to the last month, following the top performer(s) for the last 3 months is following the trend for the intermediate trend.

As of Feb., 2016, the utility index within S&P 500 has been up about 8% year-to-date while S&P 500 was down by about 8%. It is another example that the correct sector rotation is profitable.

The primary sectors are: Basic Materials, Consumer Discretionary, Consumer Staples, Energy, Financial, Health Care, Industrial, Technology and Utilities. Click the links or search from Wikipedia for description of these sectors.

https://www.fidelity.com/sector-investing/overview

We can sub divide a sector into industries. For example, Technology can be divided into Computer and Software. When computer industry is good, it does not mean software industry is also good. Some industries such as banking software can cross more than one sector.

The above links describe sectors pretty good by Fidelity with the exception of Technology, which is divided into several sectors such as Software, Computer and Telecom by Fidelity. Here are my views on the major sectors. Many vendors including IBD provide industry rankings. Here is my additional description to cover the basic sectors and some will be described in the appropriate chapters.

Consumer Staples and Discretionary

Consumer Staples are food, beverages, household products and the products we buy as necessity. They are recession-proof. The US products have demonstrated high quality and safety. With the growing middle class in developing countries such as China and India, we expect they should grow outside the USA. Currently it is not due to tariffs.

Consumer Discretionary are just the opposite.

Besides introducing the sectors and their corresponding mutual funds and ETFs, I introduce how to evaluate sectors fundamentally and technically. For beginners, skip the rest of this section.

Links

A list of sectors.
http://www.investorguide.com/sector-list.php
Check's sector analysis.
http://seekingalpha.com/article/2806655-the-stock-market-2015-a-sector-by-sector-valuation-perspective-part-1-an-overview

1   ETFs / Mutual Funds

What is an ETF

ETFs have basic differences from mutual funds: 1. Lower management expenses, 2. Trade ETFs same as stocks, and 3. Usually more diversified but not more selective than the related mutual funds such as NOBL vs FRDPX.

The major classifications of ETFs are 1. Simulating an index such as SPY, QQQ and DIA, 2. Simulating a sector such as XLE and SOXX, 3. Simulating an asset class such as GLD and SLV, 4. Simulating a country or a group of countries such as EWC and FXI, 5. Managed by a manager(s) such as ARKK, 6. Betting a market or sector to go down such as SH and PSQ, and 7. Leveraged (not recommended for beginners).

Fidelity: Index ETFs (https://www.fidelity.com/etfs/overview).

Wikipedia on ETF (http://en.wikipedia.org/wiki/Exchange-traded_fund).

List of ETFs
ETF database (Recommended): http://etfdb.com/
ETF Bloomberg: http://www.bloomberg.com/markets/etfs/
ETF Trends: http://www.etftrends.com/
A list of ETFs. Seeking Alpha.
http://etf.stock-encyclopedia.com/category/)
A list of contra ETFs (or bear ETFs)
http://www.tradermike.net/inverse-short-etfs-bearish-etf-funds/
Misc.: ETFGuide, ETFReplay
Fidelity low-cost index funds:
https://www.youtube.com/watch?v=zpKi4_IJvlY
Fidelity Annuity funds with performance data.
http://fundresearch.fidelity.com/annuities/category-performance-annual-total-returns-quarterly/FPRAI?refann=005

Other resources
Most subscription services offer research on ETFs. IBD has a strategy dedicated to ETFs and so does AAII to name a couple. Seeking Alpha

has extensive resources for ETF including an ETF screener and investing ideas. So is ETFdb.

Not all ETFs are created equal
Check their performances and their expenses.

When to use or not to use ETFs
I prefer sector mutual funds in some industries, as they have many bad stocks such as drug industry, banks, miners and insurers. Most mutual funds cannot time the market.

When you believe a sector is heading up (or contra ETF for heading down), but you do not have time to do research on specific stocks, buy an ETF for the sector; it is same for the market.

Half ETF
Taking out half of the stocks that score below the average in an index ETF could beat the same full ETF itself. I call it HETF (half the ETF). You heard it here first. After a decade, at least one company has a similar product. To illustrate, sort the expected P/E (not including stocks with negative earnings) in ascending order and only include the stocks on the first half. Add more fundamental metrics. It will take a few minutes.

Disadvantages of ETFs
- When you have two stocks in a sector ETF one good one and one bad one, the ETF treats them the same. Stock pickers would buy the one that has a better appreciation potential.
- Sometimes the return could be misleading due to stock rotation. To illustrate this, on August 29, 2012, SHLD was replaced by LYB in a sector fund. SHLD was down by 4% and LYB was up by 4% primarily due to the switch. Unless you sell and buy at the right time (which is impossible), your return would not match the ETF's returns due to the replacement.
- Ensure the performance matches the corresponding index; it is hard due to excluding dividends.

Advantages of ETFs
- We have demonstrated that you can beat the market by using market timing. Between 2000 and Nov., 2013, you only exit and reenter the market 3 times and the result is astonishing.

- It is easy to rotate a sector vs. buying/selling all of the stocks in this sector. Rotating a sector is the same as trading a stock.
- The risk is spread out, and your portfolio is diversified especially for a market ETF or buying three or more ETFs in different sectors.
- Periodically the bad stocks in most funds are replaced by better stocks.
- Eliminate the time in researching stocks.

Leveraged ETFs

I do not recommend them. Some are 2x, 3x and even higher. They're too risky for beginners. However, when you are very sure or your tested strategy has very low drawdown, you may want to use them to improve performance. Most leveraged ETFs and contra ETFs have higher fees.

My basic ETF tables

I include some contra ETFs, mutual funds and Fidelity's annuity. Some of these may be interesting to you.

ETFs and funds come and go. Some ideas and classifications are my own interpretation. Refer to ETFdb for updated information. Not responsible for any error. Check out the ETF or fund before you take any action.

Table by market cap:

Category	ETF	Mutual Funds	Fidelity's Annuity	Contra ETF	Alternate
Size:					
Large Cap	DIA	See Blend		DOG	
	SPY			SH	FXAIX VOO
	QQQ			PSQ	FNCMX
	RYH				
Blend	IWD	BEQGX			
Growth	SPYG	FBGRX			FSPGX
Value	SPYV	DOGGX			FLCOX
Dividend	NOBL	FRDPX			
	VYM				
Mid Cap			FNBSC	MYY	
Blend	MDY	VSEQX			

Growth		STDIX			
		BPTRX			
Value		FSMVX			
Small Cap			FPRGC	SBB	FSSNX
Blend	IWM	HDPSX			
Growth		PRDSX			FECGX
Value		SKSEX			FISVX
Micro	IWC				
Multi					
Blend		VDEOX			
Growth		VHCOX			
Value		TCLCX			
Total					FSKAX
Bond					
Long Term (20)	VLV	BTTTX		TBF	
Mid Term (7 – 10)	VCIT	FSTGX			
Short Term (1 – 3 yrs.)	VCSH	THOPX			
Total	BOND	PONDX			
Corp Invest Grade	VCIT	NTHEX			
High Yield (junk)	PHB	SPHIX			
Muni	MUB	Check state			
Special situation					
Buy back	PKW				

Table by sectors:

Sector	ETF	Mutual Funds	Fidelity's Annuity
Banking[1]		FSRBK	
Regional	IAT		
Bio Tech	IBB	FBIOX	
	XBI	Large	
Consumer Dis.	XLY	FSCPX	FVHAC
Consumer Staple	XLP	FDFAX	FCSAC

Finance	KIE	FIDSX	FONNC
	IYF		
Energy	XLE	FSENX	FJLLC
Energy Service		FSESX	
Gold	GLD	FSAGX	
Gold Miner	GDX	VGPMX	
Health Care	IYH	FSPHX	FPDRC
	VHT	VGHCX	
House Builder	ITB	FSHOX	
	ITB	Perform	
Industrial	IYJ	FCYIX	FBALC
Material	VAW	FSDPX	
	IYM		
Oil	USO		
Oil Service	OIH	FSESX	
Oil Exploration	XOP		
Real Estate	VNQ	FRIFX	FFWLC
REIT	VNQ		
Retail	RTH	FSRPX	
	XRT		
Regional bank	KRE	FSRBX	
Semi Conduct	SMH		
Software	XSW	FSCSX	
	IGV		
Technology	XLK	FSPTX	FYENC
	FDN	FBSOX	
		ROGSX	
Telecomm.	VOX	FSTCX	FVTAC
Transport	XTN		
	IYT		
Utilities	XLU	FSUTX	FKMSC
Wireless		FWRLX	

Footnote. [1] Also check Finance.

Table by countries outside the USA:

Country	ETF	Mutual Funds	Fidelity's Annuity	Alternate
Australia	EWA			
Brazil	EWZ			
Canada	EWC	FICDX		
China	FXI	FHKCX		
EAFE	EFA			
Emerging	VWO	FEMEX	FEMAC	FPADX
Europe	VGK	FIEUX		
Global	KXI	PGVFX		
Greece	GREK			
India	INDY	MINDX		
Indonesia	EIDO			
Latin America	ILF	FLATX		
Nordic		FNORX		
Hong Kong	EWH			
Japan	EWJ	FJPNX		
S. Africa	EZA			
S. Korea	EWY	MAKOX		
Singapore	EWS			
Taiwan	EWT			
	TUR			
United Kingdom	EWU			
Foreign:				
Combination				
Intern. Div.	IDV			FTIHX
Small Cap	SCZ			
Value	EFV			
Europe	VGK			

2   Quick analysis of ETFs

Evaluate an ETF

ETFs are a basket of stocks according to the market, a specific sector, country or a specific theme.

Yahoo!Finance used to give the P/E of an ETF. Try to get it from ETFdb.com. Enter the symbol of the ETF such as XLU, and then select Valuation. If it is below 15 and above zero, it could be a value ETF. Also, if the current price is lower than its NAV, it is sold at a discount (or premium vice versa). Compare its YTD Return to SPY's.

Alternatively, get similar info from http://www.multpl.com/. In addition, this website provides the following metrics: Shiller P/E, Price/Sales, and Price/Book.

From Finviz.com, enter the ETF symbol. If SMA-20%, SMA-50% and SMA-200% are all positive, most likely the ETF is in an uptrend. To illustrate, SMA-200 is Simple Moving Average for the last 200 trading sessions (no trading on weekends and specific holidays). The percent is how much the stock price of the ETF is above the SMA. If the percent is negative, it means the stock price is below the SMA.

If your average holding period of your stocks is about 50 days, SMA-50% is more appropriate to you.

If RSI(14) > 65, it is probably oversold; if it is < 30, it is probably under-sold (indicating value).

In addition, ensure the ETF's average volume is high (I suggest more than 10,000 shares), the market cap is more than 300 M, and it has low fees. Most popular ETFs have these characteristics. Beginners should avoid leveraged ETFs.

How to determine if the sector has been recovered

It is easier to profit by following the uptrend of an ETF using the above info. It is hard to detect when the bottom of an ETF has been reached. If SMA-20%, SMA-50% and SMA-200% are all positive, most likely the ETF is in an uptrend or it has recovered. It does not always happen as predicted, so use stops to protect your investment.

An example

First, determine whether the market is risky. Most beginners should not invest in a risky market. Advanced investors can bet against the market or a specific sector by buying contra ETFs or puts.

Next, you want to limit the number of sector ETFs by selecting those that are either in an uptrend or hitting bottom (bottom is hard to predict). Personally, I prefer sectors with long-term uptrends (indicated by articles found in many websites including cnnfn.com and Seeking Alpha.

For illustration purposes only for deteriorating market conditions, I would select the following ETFs: SPY (simulating the market based on large companies) and XLP (consumer staples). XLP should perform better than XLY (consumer discretionary) during a recession as those products are the necessities.

Technical indicators such as SMA-50 (Simple Moving Average for the last 50 sessions), SMA-200 and RSI(14) are obtained from Finviz.com and the rest are obtained from Yahoo!Finance.com. After you buy the ETF, use a stop loss to protect your investment. For example, biotech sector moved up for many months until it crashed in 2015. Change the stop loss value every month to protect your gains in this case.

As of 2/5/2016	SPY	XLP (staples)	XLY (discreet.)
Price	190	50	71
NAV	192	50	73
• Technical			
SMA-50	-4%	0%	-7%
SMA-200	-6%	2%	-7%
RSI(14)	44	50	36
Other	Double bottom at $186		
• Fundamental			
P/E	17	20	19
Yield	2.1%	2.5%	1.5%
YTD return	-5%	0.5%	-5%
Net asset	174 B	9 B	10 B

Explanation
- The figures may not be identical among websites due to the dates they are using.
- XLY has the best discount among the 3 ETFs as most investors believe a recession is coming.
- XLP has less down trend among the 3 ETFs as expected.
- XLY is more undersold among the three as expected.
- Double bottom is a technical pattern that indicates the stock would surge upward.
- SPY has a better value according to its P/E.

- XLY's dividend is the least among the three as they have more tech companies in the ETF. They have to plow back the profits to research and development.
- XLP has the best YTD return among the three.
- As long as the asset is above 500 M (200 M for specialized ETFs), it is fine and all three pass this mark.

There are many metrics such as Debt/Equity not readily available from most websites. Many sites list the top holdings of a specific ETF. Just average the metrics of the top ten or so of its stock holdings.

#Filler: Illogical logic

If we do not test for the pandemic, we would have zero increase in this pandemic. Some silly folks buy this argument. What happens to the once-great country?

Filler: The problems of the U.S.

1. Our political system. We waste time arguing between the two parties. There is no long-term planning, as the other party could claim the credit. Same as corporations' CEOs who care about their yearly bonuses.
2. The politicians have to satisfy their voters. Today give them free cash by jacking up the printing press. And ignore the long-term consequences.
3. We have to protect our workers, our environment... Hence, we cannot compete with many countries.
4. We have spent too much on the military and ignore our crumbling infrastructure.
5. Historically no country can rule the world forever.
6. We blame China, but ignore how hard-working Chinese are.

An example

This example evaluates RING, a gold miner, using ETFdb and Finviz that are free from the web. The data is from July, 6, 2020.

Bring up ETFdb and enter RING in the search. There is basic info that are important to me: Sector (gold miners), Asset Size (Large-Cap), Issuer (iShares), Inception (Jan. 31, 2012), Expense Ratio (0.39%) and Tax Form (1099).

They fit all my requirements. The expense ratio is higher than most ETFs that simulate an index such as SPY. I try to trade ETFs using Tax Form 1099 in my taxable accounts. The large cap created about 8 years ago by a reputable company is good.

Select "Dividend and Valuation". P/E of 17.39 is fine in a rank of 11 in 27 in a similar group of ETFs. As in my books, I stated it is hard to evaluate miners. I buy this ETF primarily to fight the possibility of inflation and the potential depreciation of USD. The dividend rate of 0.52% (0.70% from Finviz) is in the low range of the scale; it is fine for me as dividend is not my concern.

There is more info from this website. For simplicity, bring up Finviz:
- The short-term trend is up (SMA-20% = 8% and SMA-50% = 7%).
- The long-term trend is up (SMA-200% = 26%).
- It is close to overbought (RSI(14) = 64%; 65% to me is overbought).
- It is -4% from 52-w High. It has performed well from the YTD, Last Year, Last Quarter, Last Month and Last Week.
- It almost doubled in price from mid-March this year.
- Avg. Vol. is fine.

From ETFdb, check the Holding. It has 39 stocks, so it is quite diversified for this industry. The two top holdings are NEM (19%) and ABX (18%), which is listed as GOLD in NYSX. I also consider buying these two stocks in addition to RING. You can estimate the other metrics that are not available by averaging these two stocks. Here is my summary:

STOCK	NEM	GOLD
Forward P/E	20	25
Debt / Share	0.31	0.24
ROE	17%	22%
Sales Q/Q	43%	30%
EPS Q/Q	389%	254%
SMA50	2%	4%
RSI(14)	59%	60%
Insider Trans	-13%	N/A
Fidelity's Equity Summary Score	6.1	6.8

3   Sectors to be cautious with

There are many reasons to be very cautious when investing in the following sectors. However, Technical Analysis (a.k.a. charting) would give you more hints than the fundamentals for stocks in these sectors.

Loan companies/banks

The financial statements do not show the quality of their loan portfolios. Banks should make easy money when you compare the CD rates to the mortgage rates. However, they could lose money in the following: 1. Default of loans / mortgages that happen frequently during recessions. 2. Banks are making risky investments that fail such as Bitcoins. 3. Investing in losing vehicles, such as the 'safe' Treasuries during rapid interest hikes (happened in 2023). 4. Poor management and/or frauds. Following this advice, you may be able to skip the banks that melted down in 2007. The peak of Citigroup was $550 and several banks including Lehman Brothers went bankrupt.

To protect ourselves, do not have one bank account with our assets over $250,000, which is protected by FDIC. Be careful on foreign banks, especially the small ones and those that are not protected by FDIC.
https://www.youtube.com/watch?v=qmpVABboOKQ

Failure of Silicon Valley Bank in 2023. If Biden did not mention about paying deposits back in full (many companies have deposits more than the insured amount), it would have shaken our financial system and the entire economic system. The failure is partly due to the rapid interest rates hikes and partly due to the loss of the loans from startup companies in a slowdown in the tech sector. Any unlawful insider trading? Be cautious on small banks; in 2008, about 1/3 of the small banks failed. I expect money from small banks would move to precious metals and larger banks.
https://www.youtube.com/watch?v=atlyLIP9sFs

Drug (generic is ok)

Understanding the complexities of the drug pipelines, its potential profits for new drugs and the expiration of its current drugs may not be worth the effort for most retail investors. In addition, a serious lawsuit and / or a serious problem with a drug could wipe out a good percentage of the stock price. When a drug shows unpromising sign(s) in any trial phase, the stock could plunge and vice versa.

Miners It is extremely difficult to estimate how much ore (sometimes a miner owns several different types of ores and/or of different grades in the same or different mines) that the company has. It is further complicated by the complexities to extract and transport them. When the total of these costs is greater than its production price, the company will not be profitable. Understanding the market for ore futures is another discipline.

Many mining companies are in foreign countries such as Canada, Australia and countries in South America. Their financial statements of Canada and Australia are more trustworthy than those from most other emerging countries.

One potential problem of mining companies from many emerging countries is nationalization.

Mining rare earth ore is extremely risky when the profit depends on how China, a major producer of these ores, will price its ores. After China announced the export restrictions on rare earth elements, several non-Chinese companies announced to reopen their mines for rare earths but few have made any profits as of 2013. Developed countries have stricter environmental regulations. Coal suffers from the rising use of cleaner oil and gas.

Insurance companies
Insurance companies profit by:

1. The difference between the total premiums received and the total claims minus expenses in running the company.
2. How well they invest your premiums; you pay your premiums earlier than you may collect from the claims.

They can protect the profits in #1 by restricting claims by natural disasters such as earthquakes and by re-insuring. However, a bad disaster could wipe out a lot of their profits.
Even if the insurance company shows you its investment portfolio, most of us, the retail investors, do not have the time and expertise to analyze it.

Emerging countries (not a sector)
Their financial statements especially from small companies cannot be trusted and many countries use different accounting standards. Emerging countries are where the economic growth is. I trade FXI, an ETF, rather than individual Chinese companies. I have lost a lot in small Chinese companies due to fraud. To check out whether the stock is an ADR, try ADR.COM.
https://www.adr.com/

Stocks with low volumes (not a sector) Most likely you pay a high spread to trade these stocks. They can be manipulated easier. I remember when I had a hard time trying to sell a stock of this kind. The majority of this company is owned by one person.

For simplicity, I trade stocks with the average daily trade volume over 6,000 shares (double it if the price is $2 or less). A better way could be in calculating the percent of your trade quantity / average daily trade volume to reduce the effect of penny stocks that have larger volumes due to the low prices. You need special skills to trade these stocks but it could be very profitable.

Good business and bad business
Banking is a good business. My deposit in them makes virtually zero interest, and they loan the same money making 3%. If they are more selective in loaning my money, they should make a good profit.

Restaurant is an easy business to open/run, but it is very hard to make good money. With the rising of minimal wages, it will get even tougher. That could be the reason for so many coupons today. The high-end restaurants are doing better due to the rising stock market. As of 8/2014, the newcomers Noodles & Company (NDLS) and Potbelly (PBPB) are not doing very well.

Retailing is a tough business. Looking at the top 10 retailers 15 years ago, I can only find two including Macy's that are still surviving. Most are either bankrupt or being acquired. Even Macy's was at one time in financial trouble.

Airlines are a tough business. You can tell by the average increase in fares in the last 10 years. It cannot even beat inflation. They have to charge you for everything. The next frontier charge is the restroom (especially for long-distance flights). Now I understand why they call themselves "Frontier Airline". As of 2014, it is quite profitable due to mergers and lower fuel cost.

There are several software companies that produce software such as virus detecting programs and tax preparation software. The customers faithfully buy new versions every year. That's great business.

Links
Nationalization: http://en.wikipedia.org/wiki/Nationalization
Spread: http://en.wikipedia.org/wiki/Bid-offer_spread
Insurance:http://seekingalpha.com/article/1239671-property-casualty-insurance-and-reinsurance-what-you-need-to-know

4 TA for sector rotation, reentry & peak

There are 3 uses of TA for sector rotation.

1. Detect sector plunge and when to reenter the market after plunges.
2. Regular use (usually after its recovery from a plunge).
3. Detect market plunges and/or sector plunges.

#3 has been described on the chapter Spotting Market Plunges and it will not be repeated here.

The difference in #1 and #2 is in the number of days in SMA (Single Moving Average). Use 350 for sector plunge and reentry.

Use 30, 60, 90 or 120 for regular use (i.e. after the reentry from a market plunge) depending on how frequently you rotate. If you rotate in 60 days, use 60 for the average of number of days.

Exit / Reenter a sector ETF

To illustrate, the following example uses XHB (an ETF for the housing sector). Use the same chart for other sector ETFs such as VGK for Europe.

Produce the following chart by using Yahoo!Finance. Enter XHB and select Interactive Chart. Select SMA and then 350 days. Select Max for 'From'.

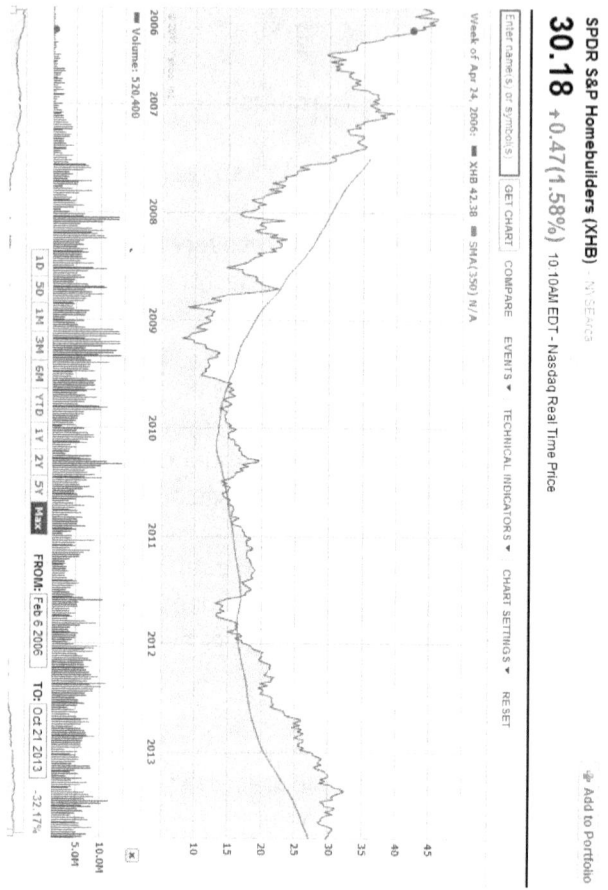

Source: Yahoo!Finance. XHB on 350 SMA.

- Exit when the price falls below the red, single-moving average (the SMA) and enter when it is over the SMA. All the dates and prices are approximate and for illustration only.

- I use Max for the period. Let's assume the chart instructed us to exit at $45 around 2006 and reenter on August, 2009 missing a loss of about $30 per share. Not too bad!

- There are brief exits and reentries before 2012. I call it noises. The gains and losses are negligible. However, make sure you exit and also reenter. If you use 60 days instead of 350 days in this example, you have more noises. If you trade the ETF more often, then you use 60 or 90 days. It depends on your risk tolerance and your time to trade. Sometimes the performance makes a difference in selecting shorter days, but not all the time.

- From the end of 2012 to today (10-2013), it gains more than 40% compared to -32% for the period for buy-and-hold. A difference of 62%! Even a difference of 10% would be great.

- The chart works at least for this period. It is every one's guess whether it will still work in the future. I bet it will but as in life nothing is guaranteed.

- When a housing stock, the housing sector (XHB) and the general stock market all above their respective SMAs, the stock most likely will appreciate (again nothing is guaranteed).

- From my other chapters, the offending sector (housing and finance for 2007 market plunge) takes about two years to recover from the bottom.

  I interpreted the bottom was 10-2007, so the recovery would start in 10-2009. If you bought XHB in 10-2009, you would have gained about 100% today (10-22-2013).

- Some sectors never recover such as the internet and some high-tech companies in 2000.

Now, it is your turn to try out the chart. This time, use 60 for the number of days in SMA.

Afterthoughts
- We have discussed how to use TA to spot market crashes and individual stocks. TA can help us to determine a sector. For my purpose, I usually use 90-day moving average on an ETF for that industry, but 350-day moving average for detecting sector plunges / reentries.
- The big boys (hedge fund managers) moved their money into GOOG and AMZN solely to make a ton of cash when AAPL reached $700 and they will move their investment out of AMZN (too high value as of 1-2013) or GOOG back into AAPL.

Instead of fighting the big movers, join them by using the tool of TA. Make good money by winning the second place of a horse race.

- A stock will always go up and down for more than several days in a row. Take advantage of the trend and make some quick money if you are a short-term trader.
- If all the following are above the single moving average (SMA) line, most likely (most and not all) the stock price will rise in next month:

  1. 350-day SMA of SPY (representing the market).
  2. 60-day (or 90-day) SMA of the sector ETF that represents the sector the stock is in.
  3. 30-day SMA (or 20 for some folks) of the stock and it passes our (or your) scoring system.

  Most technicians use 20, 50 and 200 days for moving averages for stocks. To save you time, use finviz.com to obtain the % of the stock deviates from its moving averages. When it is positive, it is usually a buy.
- A book mentioned to me on TA: Stan Weinstein's book, "Secrets for Profiting in Bull & Bear Markets".
- If you are a customer of Fidelity, try the option to include all indicators in charting a stock. To illustrate of using index S&P 500, use .SPX (^GSPC in Yahoo!Finance).
- Sectors can also be divided by market cap. Use the same charts to find the trend of small cap for example.
- When TA tells you to sell a stock, try to find the reasons by using google, SeekingAlpha, Yahoo!Finance board, calling the company, etc.
- More related articles.

Based on performance.
http://stockcharts.com/help/doku.php?id=chart_school:trading_st rategies:sector_rotation_roc
Fidelity.
https://www.fidelity.com/learning-center/trading-investing/markets-sectors/sector-rotation-introduction
A subscription service.
http://www.sectortimingreport.com/articles/sector-rotation.html

Strategy 4: Momentum investing

Introduction

This strategy provides me with steady income by working an hour or two every week. How long will it last? I do not know. I will describe the concept here, so you can devise your own to fit your risk tolerance and requirements.

As of this writing, this strategy is having amazing returns. Though these returns may not be sustainable, my convictions are so strong that I am boldly increasing my investment. When the market is trending up, this strategy is very profitable particularly if the stocks are in the rising sectors. When the market is trending down, find the worst stocks and short them.

The concept of a momentum strategy

Each week, I buy about 5 stocks based on the momentum metrics and sell them within a month. I do not use the fundamental metrics a lot, as that will not be effective in such a short duration. From my current record, the average holding time is about 20 days.

The details of my strategy will not be disclosed fully but the concept is. When a strategy is used too often, it will not be effective and would end up churning the same stocks for all its followers. However, let me elaborate on the implementation of this momentum strategy and give you some ideas on how to build one for yourself.

My Theory. When a stock is on the uptrend, most likely it will continue for at least for a week or two. Do not buy stocks when the market is risky. Protect yourself by using stops and / or using technical indicators such as SMA-20 (Simple Moving Average).

Subscription services

I spent less than half an hour finding about 6 stocks to buy. My choice is helped by subscription services. Some have earnings revision information (particularly useful during earnings seasons) and most others have provided timing grades. I include the insider purchase information and short-term technical indicators. It works so far and I constantly monitor the performance.

For starters, use simple screens and procedures to find stocks without getting a subscription service. Paper trade your screens and strategies to include your average holding period and money management before you commit to use real money.

Common parameters

I subscribe to several investment services and select their recommendations. From my recent reviews, I only need a good subscription with a historical database plus the free Fidelity, Yahoo!Finance and Finviz. Most of these sites provide a timing ranking. The rank for value should take a back seat in momentum stocks.

To illustrate, the composite rank for timing in Blue Chip Growth (not free any more) is the Quantitative Score. It is also known as the buying pressure. Fidelity provides similar rankings.

http://navelliergrowth.investorplace.com/bluechip/password/index.php?plocation=%2Fbluechip%2F.

There are several common parameters on how they rank stocks. These parameters may be obtained from Finviz.com.

- Price momentum. I prefer to use SMA20% (20-day simple moving average). The higher the percentage, the better. However, they should not be too high (say greater than 15%). When it is peaking, the stock may fall.

- Change of short %. Favorable if it is over 25% (for short squeezes) and unfavorable if it is moving up (say from 5% to 15%). You need to keep track of the previous short percentages for the stocks you follow.

- Sales momentum (Sales Q/Q) and earnings momentum (EPS Q/Q or quarter earnings to quarter prior year). The higher, the better.

- Earnings revisions. Zacks (free for a single stock) has good info based on their estimates and rumors.

- Insider's Purchase. No one knows the company better than its officers. You can find the Insider Transaction from Finviz.

- Analysts' recommendation. It can be obtained from Finviz.com. However, Fidelity's Equity Summary Score provides a better one and it is based on the past performances of the analysts' predictions.

- Most momentum stocks are either in technology / pharmacy or formula sectors such as Walmart using the same formula in opening stores. Many of them no longer qualify as momentum stocks when they grow too big and/or their markets are fully exploited; most of them pay dividends.

- I usually keep them for a month. However, some big winners continue even after three months. To protect your portfolio, use stop orders (trailing stops are preferred); I prefer 20% as these stocks are usually more volatile.

- Aggressive investors can sell short on stocks having negative momentum.

Reduce Taxes

I use my Roth accounts to minimize my taxes. There are many tax advantages of a Roth account. The second choice is other retirement accounts. I converted some of my Roll-Over IRA to my Roth as allowed. Consult your tax lawyer or CPS for updated information about your individual situations.

Reduce losses during market downfall

My strategy works best in the up market as I seldom short stocks. However, a major market downfall could wipe out all profits for years. In 2019, I was shorting stocks more often as the market was risky.

These are two Technical Analysis tools to anticipate a market downfall. Minimize losses once a downfall of the market has been spotted.

- Do not buy any stock.

- Sell any existing positions and/or use stops to reduce further losses.

- Aggressive investors should buy contra ETFs such as DOG, SH and PSQ (against the corresponding indexes DOW, the S&P 500 and NASDAQ) when the market is too risky. It is like buying insurance (hedging your portfolio). However, do not be the entire farm.

- Be disciplined. Most likely, your strategy should be profitable despite its ups and downs of the market especially in the long run.

- Be emotionally detached. As of 4/2013, my average annualized return of 66 round-trip trades was 127%. It is so far so good, but it will not be sustainable in the longer run. I do expect some losses.

- Take a break from time to time. I have stopped this strategy for a while due to the risky market and taking a long vacation.

Monitor performance

I constantly monitor my metrics and my screens for performance. I am always looking at perfecting better systems and /or adapting to the current market conditions.

- Day of the week.
  Monday is not a good day to find stocks. Most of my subscriptions do not update their information on weekends, and the prices are the same as last Friday. I try not to trade on Fridays as I hate to leave unexecuted orders over the weekend.

- Reduce the number of stocks.

Usually, I have an average of eight stocks for further analysis each time, and I select the five stocks or less after evaluation.

- Listen to the experts.
  If all the timing grades from different subscription services are high for a specific stock, the appreciation potential of this stock should be high

- Maximize profit.
  If this strategy proves itself and the market is not risky, I'll increase my position and vice versa.

- Improve performance and reduce risk.
  I have found that about 10% of the gains were due to good timing. If the purchased stock appreciates more than my target price, I sell it right away. My average holding period in this period is about 20 days and the gain is about 3% (the annualized return is huge due to the short average duration).

  From my limited data so far, holding stocks for 20 days gives them better performance rather than holding them longer than 60 days.

- Calculating the rate of return.
  I prefer the annualized rate of return for a better comparison. However, I would skip using those performances from trades with the holding period less than five days. I also compare my return to the return of S&P 500 on the same holding period.

  The better rate to calculate the rate of return is: Total Profit / Total Investment. We have cash between trades. It is too time-consuming for most.

- Money management.
  In a rising market, usually too much idle cash (due to taking profits) would decrease the performance of the portfolio and vice versa in a falling market.

  In a falling or risky market, limit your stock holding exposure to market risk. Instead of holding the stocks for a month, try to sell them in a week or two, and increase your cash position. You need cash to buy stocks when the market returns.

- If you do not use market orders, try to place the order price as close as the last executed price in the market. I usually submit orders after 10 am; they call the first hour (9:30 am to 10:30 am in NYC) the amateur hour for a good reason.

- My purchase prices are usually about a little less (.2%) than the market prices and sometimes even lower especially when the market is trending downward.

  When the stock is trending up, there is a good chance my purchase order is not executed. I summed up the potential profits lost and the money I saved from the discounts in my purchase prices. It turns out they even like each other. In several instances, the stocks just rocket upwards. If I cannot buy the stock after 4 or so hours, I should switch the buy order to market order.

- I prefer to beat the market by a smaller margin but more consistently.

- Using a trading plan makes it a discipline and avoids emotional influences.

Recent (4/2016) examples

Recently there were two coaster-roller stocks: Fitbits and GPro. Both stock prices surged through the roof and crashed down. Using the "Buy High and Sell Higher" strategy should have made you some money if you protected your profit via trailing stops.

The momentum is caused by the publicity and the public who follow the trend blindly. The fundamentals of both companies when they were rising, they did not justify the prices. It is like buying a hot dog cart in NYC for a million dollars. Of course, you will sell a lot of hot dogs as long as you do not have another hot dog cart next to your cart. However, your investment may never be recouped. In addition, both are single-product companies; it would be very risky when there is competition. Apple is one for Fitbits and

I bet many Chinese companies are making products similar to GPro's. GPro's products could be a fad, or they may fall into a limited, specialized market.

Ignore fundamentals for momentum stocks. Ride on the bandwagon and jump off when the trend reverses.

Afterthoughts
There are several SA articles on similar topic, click here, here and here.
The links are:
http://seekingalpha.com/article/1336291-does-momentum-investing-actually-work?v=1365785958&source=tracking_notify
http://seekingalpha.com/article/865091-how-price-momentum-and-bull-markets-go-together?source=kizur
http://seekingalpha.com/article/1350651-seeking-alpha-momentum-investing-with-etfs

#Filler
Percentage wise, my momentum investing has been most profitable so far. I classify this strategy into 3 sub strategies depending on the average durations.

1   My momentum performance

The following includes all the actual transactions from September, 2013 to Dec., 2013 in my momentum portfolio. "Lot Date" is the day I evaluate what stocks to buy. Some stocks are bought on different days after the evaluation and some are not bought. I am not responsible for any errors in preparing the following tables.

Lot Date	Stock	Buy Date	Days	Ann. %
09/04/13	BOFI	09/04/13	6	(175%)
	GMCR	09/04/13	14	110%
	Z	09/04/13	6	40%
	FB	09/05/13	8	419%
	AFOP	09/04/13	6	353%
	EGAN	09/04/13	5	194%
	PB	09/06/13	10	78%
09/11/13	ARWR	09/12/13	12	136%
	CATM	09/13/13	4	136%
	GILD	09/13/13	6	157%
	YELP	09/11/13	6	242%
	TRN	09/13/13	32	24%
09/24/13	AFOP	09/26/13	22	(105%)
	DRYS	09/24/13	81	15%
	PACB	09/28/13	20	(258%)
10/02/13	ZLC	10/02/13	14	293%
	FB	10/02/13	15	20%
10/05/13	DYAX	10/08/13	16	(109%)
	FSS	10/08/13	31	160%
10/18/13	GERN	10/18/13	21	1176%
	ALGN	10/22/13	48	(22%)
	COBZ	10/22/13	62	108%
	WAL	10/18/13	21	103%
	LCI	10/22/13	10	434%
	AKRX	10/31/13	15	334%
	BREW	11/01/13	7	194%
	BCEI	10/22/13	10	434%
	RAD	10/22/13	41	142%
11/05/13	LCC merged	11/06/13	3	639%
	TRN	11/08/13	63	41%
	CIR	11/05/13	43	21%
11/12/13	LCI	11/12/13	38	138%
	TRN	11/12/13	3	785%
	UBNT	11/12/13	3	1461%
	LCC	11/12/13	61	20%
	FCN	11/12/13	38	(12%)
11/19/13	FOE	11/19/13	35	(6%)
	NUVA	12/11/13	9	93%

11/25/13	GTN	12/03/13	3	1289%
	CRY	11/26/13	49	39%
	ARC	11/26/13	24	(85%)
	BONT	12/20/13	25	(344%)
12/03/13	AIRM	12/03/13	17	44%
	FIX	12/03/13	20	(97%)
12/10/13	MDXG	12/19/13	8	1162%
	MPAA	12/16/13	7	(7%)
	LBMH	12/14/13	6	627%
	UVE	12/11/13	12	48%
	USAK	12/10/13	13	(18%)
	ARC	12/10/13	13	(144%)
	CONN	12/12/13	11	55%
	REI	12/10/13	10	192%
		Biggest loss		(344%)
		Average		200%

My best profitable month

All the stocks purchased have been sold. Some stocks were bought twice in another account and they may have been at different prices/holding durations. Stopped this strategy in 2019 due to the risky market, but will return when the market is less risky. In 2019, I switched to shorting stocks. Jan., 2014 was one of my best months then.

Lot Date	Stock	Buy Date	Days	Ann. %
01/14/14	LCI	01/14/14	30	85%
	ENDP	01/16/14	42	140%
	LCI	01/14/14	38	208%
	NSTG	01/14/14	56	36%
	BABY	01/26/14	35	156%
	NSTG	01/14/14	59	34%
	ZNGX	01/21/14	31	133%
01/22/14	ANIP	01/22/14	29	195%
	KS	01/22/14	33	115%
	CHIP	01/22/14	19	246%
	SLXP	01/22/14	33	77%
	GMCR	01/22/14	20	743%
		Biggest loss		34%
		Average		181%

Explanation

- Lot Date. I usually group the stocks I buy by weeks. When I have losses two times in a row, I would buy fewer stocks or even skip purchase altogether.

  I try to maintain a total balance for this portfolio. I would buy fewer stocks when the balance is close to this threshold. As of 3/15/14, the market is too risky (plunging or peaking), and hence I would not buy any momentum stocks. When the market falls, these momentum stocks will fall faster and steeper than the rest of the market.

- I started this momentum portfolio far earlier, but I only recorded it recently. I took a long summer break in 2013 and resumed it in September, 2013 (the start date of the first table).

  There are some positions not sold after Dec., 2013. Anyway, I have enough data for illustration purposes. Most likely, the reason for showing any 'unclosed' positions is due to housekeeping errors, not trying to present a better result than what may appear.

- I did not include the stocks that have not been bought due to my lower buy prices and/or not meeting my criteria of what to buy. When any of my subscription services tells me the stock is not a buy, I skip it. A few times, some recommended stocks just skyrocketed in prices in the open. I did not buy most if not all of these stocks.

- I've averaged the returns for the above tables. The first table has a 200% annualized return while the second one has 181%.

  However, the actual profit of this portfolio is far better in the second table – most likely due to some larger position sizes. The higher annualized return in the first table is due to shorter durations. In my actual monitor, I ignore the returns if they are less than five days, as they distort the returns.

- The actual performance should be worse due to not considering the idle cash. I also excluded the contra ETFs to hedge the portfolio. In 2013, the hedging was a losing game in a rising market. Dividends were not considered in calculating the returns.

- The better way is to compare the performances with the S&P 500 index, which is too time-consuming for me.

- My holding period is short. With many exceptions, I sell these stocks within a month or they have appreciated a lot.

- You can have a portfolio for momentum stocks and another one for value stocks.

- MTUM an ETF for momentum stocks. COWZ is an ETF for cash cows.

From my book series "Best Stocks", the performances of my recommended momentum stocks.

Book	Stocks	Return	Ann.	Beat RSP by
Best stocks to buy for 2022	5	99%	4%	4,475%
Best Stocks to buy as of July, 2021	2	12%	137%	265%
Best Stocks for 2021 2nd Edition	7	-3%	35%	-170%

The details can be found in the following link.
http://tonyp4idea.blogspot.com/2022/12/best-stocks-series.html

2   Five strategies for momentum

We have 3 strategies according to the different holding periods. The screen parameters (i.e., selection criteria) are briefly described here. Adjust them to fit your risk tolerance and requirements. Monitor them from time to time as the market always changes. Finviz does not provide most metrics for Strategy #4. Strategy #5 is a combination of the first 3 strategies and will be described separately.

Metric	Strategy #1	Strategy #2	Strategy #3	Strategy #4
Avg. holding period	< 30 days	60 days	90 days	30 to 90 days
General				
Market Cap	300 M – 2 B	300 M – 2B	2B – 10B	> 200
Avg. volume	>100K	>200K	> 300 K	> 80.000
Analyst Rec[1]	Buy or better	Buy or better	Buy or better	
Country	USA	USA	USA	USA
Price	>$5	>$10	>$10	>$1
Insider Purchases	Positive	Positive	Positive	Positive
Fundamental				
P/E	>0	>0	>0	
Forward P/E	>0	>0	>0	
Return on Equity		>10%	>10%	
EPS Growth next year		>15%	>10%	>20%
Sales Growth rate				5%
Technical				
Performance	Week up	Week up	Week up	

SMA-20%	> 5%			
SMA-50%	> 0%	>2%		>SMA-200%
SMA-200%	>0%	>0%	>0%	

[1] I usually do not care about fundamentals for momentum stocks.

In addition, they should be in one of the 3 major exchanges: NYSEX, NASDAQ and AMEX (Finviz.com allows you to select one exchange at a time).

In general, Strategy #1 does not care about fundamentals. Strategy #2 is a typical sector rotation candidate. Strategy #3 cares more about fundamentals.

I recommend paper trading your strategy using different selection criteria. When you are comfortable, commit a small amount of cash and increase your portfolio size gradually.

Vendors

Most services charge a fee. However, many free sites provide momentum (same as timing) score. Most have a score (same as rank and grade) for timing. Usually, they are based on the momentum of the price. If the price jumps very fast and high, this score is high. Use stops to protect your profits. When the price is below a set price (such as 10% from your purchase price), use a market order to sell it. When the timing score is the highest, be very cautious as it cannot go any higher, or a peak is close.

Example

Here is an example of how to find the momentum stocks for your portfolio.

Bring up Finviz.com. Select Screener. Select 20-Day Simple Moving Average above 20%. Sort the screened stocks with this parameter. Today I have about 100 stocks.

Limit your selection to fit your requirements and preferences. Here are some sample criteria: U.S. companies only, capital cap over 100 M, price over $2 and relative volume over 1. Ignore ETFs.

Check whether the screened stocks are peaking (say they have appreciated over 100%) and/or overbought (RSI(14) > 65). Check the reasons for recent surges and evaluate whether the momentum would continue or not. Check out any insider purchases at prices close to market prices.

Strategy #5

This is a variation of the described in the first three strategies. I explain it with a step-by-step approach in implementing it using Finviz.com. Bring it up by typing Finviz.com in your browser. In addition, super stocks usually are small stocks by market cap with small float and high volatility (high beta that can be found in Finviz). Strategy #5: Buy stocks whose SMA-5 is higher than SMA-20 and exit otherwise.

1. Only buy momentum stocks when the market is not risky. When the tide is up, all ships will flow up. Check out my market timing technique. In the simplest way, enter SPY (or any ETF that simulates the market) in Finviz.com. If SMA-20%, SMA-50% and SMA-200% are all positive, most likely the market is not risky. 20% is more important than the other two.
2. Screen. The following are my preferred metrics and you can change them to suit your requirements and risk tolerance.

   From the Descriptive tab, Select Small (300M to 2B) for Market Cap, Over 100K for Average Volume, Over 2 for Relative Volume, USA for Country and Over $5 for Price. Repeat it for other ranges such as 100M to 4B in the Market Cap. For 100 M market cap, use over $1 for Price; increase the price for larger market cap such as using 'over $2' for 200 M market cap.
3. From Fundamental tab, select Positive in Insider Transaction.
4. From Technical tab, select 10% above SMA-50 in SMA-20 (Simple Moving Average for the last 20 days) and 20% above 200-SMA in SMA-50. If you have too many stocks, reduce the 10% to 8% or less. Change the selection if they are not desirable for you and/or the current market conditions.

   As of 11/07/2016, I have the following 4 stocks: AAOI, BOOT, LC and NILE. They already had good price increases.
5. Click on the selected stocks one by one such as AAOI. From most other metrics, it is not a value stock. The Forward P/E is 16. Hence, it has some value despite the high P/E of 80. All SMA%s are positive which indicate it is trending up.

6. After you bought the stock, use stop loss to limit any losses especially in this risky market. Conservative investors should stay away from risky markets. I would set a 15% stop loss (i.e., sell it via a market order when it loses 15%).

7. Most likely you will not or cannot buy a stock via a discount price when the stock is trending up.

8. Save the screen with a name such as Momentum, so you do not have to reenter the metrics again.

9. Finviz does not provide a historical database. You can run the test every week (or monthly) and write down the results. Only invest with real money when you're comfortable with your tests. If your expected maximum loss is 50%, double your portfolio size as the money you can afford to lose.

10. Making 55% profitable trades could be very profitable.

11. There are many variations and parameters to this strategy such as RSI(14), Double Bottom in Pattern and New High in 52-Week High/Low.

12. If your purchased stock is moving up, review it every month (preferable every week) and set up a trailing stop. To illustrate, when it is up by 20%, set the stop at the current price (not the price you paid for the stock).

13. From a trader guru: 1. Test and select the strategy suitable for your personality and risk tolerance. 2. Learn from mistakes. 3. Select and buy from the best stocks, vice versa for shorting. 4. Protect your loss and let profits rise. 5. Diversify. 6. Reevaluate the strategy and the acquired stocks. 7. Consider the business cycle and the market cycle. 8. Stocks with prices between 1 to 10 are better for trading as most analysts do not follow them.

Link: Swing: https://www.youtube.com/watch?v=C9EQkA7uVU8
Momentum: https://www.youtube.com/watch?v=PpUlOyZrl9

Filler: Black swan

No EU countries want the war in Ukraine for their own benefits. No politicians, even comedians, want to confront an enemy with tanks at the gate. It turns a rich country into the poorest country in the region.

3   Herd theory

When the herd makes money, they think they're a genius. The last one to leave the herd will be the fool of all fools such as the last holders of Lehman Brothers, AIG, Bear Stearns, internet stocks in 2000, etc. The biggest fools are the 'value' buyers when these companies were plunging fast. When a specific stock looked great yesterday and it lost 50% today, it 'must' be super good to some. Wrong! Check out why it plunged. It could be missing some important metric, or something is really wrong with the company that   did   not   show   up   in   the   research.

The real genius is the one who makes money all the way up, but leaves before the bubble bursts. Even a genius cannot predict the peak and the bottom, but I'll call him/her a genius if s/he is right better   than   60%   of   the   time.

Recently dividend growth stocks have the highest premium in the last 30 years. It is a mild bubble when we've many retired, or retiring folks seeking income. However, the bubble will burst when the interest rates rise. At that time, the long-term bonds with low yields will lose.

Dividend stocks will benefit when the interest rates are low. Bond holders would move to dividend stocks from their low-yield bonds. Long-term bonds lose their value when the interest rates rise, and vice   versa.

It is the same for the internet bubble in 2000. I did unload most of my tech funds in early April, 2000. The more I read during that time, the more I got scared. It was partly luck and partly 'genius' to move all these sector funds to traditional industries. At that time, they did not have contra ETFs, so cash, money market funds and bonds would be the best choices.

Filler
Had you responded to the pandemic, which was confirmed on Feb., 2020? If you do, you should have shorted stocks on airline, cruise line and related sectors, or at least bought contra ETS (the market returned after the big dip due to the excessive printing of money). After the excessive printing of money, we would have bought ETFs related to gold such as GLD and RING.

4   Characteristics of momentum trading

- Usually the beta (from Finviz) is higher than 1 (the average). The higher the price fluctuation, the better for momentum stocks.

- Market caps of most momentum stocks are higher than 1B. Institutional investors move the market. However, many of my big gainers are smaller stocks; it could be due to my small bet positions.

- The 4 phases of a stock: neglect, growing, peaking and plunging. Buy at the 'growing' phase. In the 'neglect' stage, you may spot bargains, but the stock would stay in this stage for a long while. Most of the time, the stock fluctuates around 200-SMA. When the volume is high in trending up and low in pullbacks, this stock may be in stage 2, a buying opportunity.

- Do not be afraid of the daily surge of the price. Sometimes, you have to pay close to the market price for a rising stock.

- Do not sell your winners too early. Watch out for exceptions and use stops or trailing stops to protect your portfolio.

- Sell in phase 3 with the characteristics: price below 200-SMA (from Finviz), Volume higher in a losing day and lower in a profiting day and Large loss after earnings announcement.

- Do not listen and follow the financial news. A lot of time, the news has been fabricated to serve the purpose of the analysts.

- From my experience, many times the insiders are wrong. Most likely they do not study the trend as described in this book.

- Do the exact opposite for shorting stocks.

5   Good News/Bad News

This is a version of the "Buy high, sell higher" strategy. It responds to the news. Hence, it is faster and it could complete the trade in a few days or even a day.

If you started on the day Trump announced the tariff and lasted today (4/2018), you should make some good money. You buy SPY (or similar ETF) when there is bad news and sell (and buy contra ETFs for more speculative traders) when there is good news such as China's announcement on negotiating trade retaliation.

You should adjust the strategy to your individual risk tolerance. In any case, use trailing stops to protect losses. To illustrate, buy SPY when it is 1% down and double the bet when it is 2% down.

This strategy will not work when there is a defined trend such as heading to a market crash. As always, practice the strategy not with real money until you're comfortable.

Recent news
When it happens, have you prepared yourself to take advantage of the situation? Aggressive investors can short stocks and/or ETFs specific to the situation.

- Pandemic. Actions: Sell casino stocks (esp. those in Macau), airlines, hotels, restaurants and stocks related to traveling. Buy related drug companies related to vaccines, cures and test kits.
- Trade war and delisting of China stocks. Actions: Sell Chinese stocks; I did not and I was guilty as charged. Buy when they hit bottoms (hard to detect). I bought BABA.
- Ukraine war. Actions: Buy gold and energy stocks.
- Market fluctuation and mostly down. Buy when the market is down and sell when the market is up for a volatile market. If it is confirmed to be down (detected via market timing such as death cross), sell most stocks.

6   Business news

Business news affects the momentum of stocks and sectors. We can get daily business news from many sources. Seeking Alpha's "Wall Street Breakfast" and "Trending News" are free. The following news are also available: "Latest News" in Market Watch, Bloomberg's "Bloomberg Opinion Today" Barron's "Premarket Screener", and many others. Several websites identify stocks with recent high trade volume.

Evaluate the news. I prefer to skip the news from TV and the 'gurus' who may have their own agendas. To illustrate, the tension in the Middle East, would lead to the surge of oil price and gold price. There are many other examples such as pandemic affecting the cruise and airline sectors. Evaluate the mentioned stocks and/or related sector fundamentally and technically.

Timing is everything. Most of the time, the news is old and we may miss the opportunity. Many times we may be too ahead. In this case, I would invest about 25% of the average position and then add gradually if the news is affecting the stock or sector profitably.

Use stop orders to protect your trades. You should make good money in the long run by cutting losses early and let your winners rise.

#Filler: Silence is golden

I am glad I did not give advice to a friend who had to decide whether to take a lump sum payment or an annuity. The correction in March, 2020 would wipe out a lot of his portfolio if he took the lump sum payment. No one would share his profits when the predictions are correct, but the blame if it does not materialize.

It is the same in investing that nothing is certain. With educated guesses, we should have more rights than wrongs especially in the long run.

7   Rocket stocks

There are stocks making yearly highs and continue to do so for a while. They defy fundamental rules. Among many examples, Tesla appreciated about 400% from 4/2013 to 10/2013. However, when they reverse direction, they may lose more than they have gained. BBRY lost 95% of its value in 4 years after gaining about 30 times in 5 years. Some are manipulated by institutional investors. Most have new products that could change the world. When they have unfixable problems such as competing products and/or major pending lawsuits, they will tend to plunge. I call them rocket stocks and they may plunge at the speed they surge.

From my tests on these stocks, they share common metrics. Most of these stocks are hitting 52-week highs or close to them, and they can be found in your stock section of the newspaper and many investing sites. Usually their SMA-50% is higher than their SMA-200%, which are both available from Finviz.com.

The other metrics are stock prices greater than $10 and the market cap is between 3 billion and 8 billion. I would also include 100M to 500M stocks for a larger appreciation potential although they are riskier. They should be listed in the major 3 exchanges. These are the stocks institutional investors would evaluate (greater than 4B); institutional investors drive the market. The volume should be at least double the average volume; it is a confirmation. Their rating grade on timing from many investing sites (some are free) are high.

You can alter the above criteria especially on many small drug companies and small high-tech companies. Insider purchases are another good criterion to search for rocket stocks. Avoid bankrupting stocks no matter how high they surge.

Do not be greedy as some will return to the original prices and even go to zero. When the institutional investors switch to the next rocket stock or sector, these rocket stocks will plunge in their prices. As recommended on how to sell rising stocks, use mental (a.k.a. trailing) stops such as 10%. When it falls to 10% of the last time you set the stop, sell it and **do not look back**. The average holding period of 3 months is the best in my limited testing. However, some rocket stocks do not obey the law of gravity. No one can time the peaks and bottoms consistently. Never buy a growth stock in a downward trend.

Link: 52-week high:
https://www.barchart.com/stocks/highs-
lows/highs?timeFrame=1y

8   FAANG stocks

To many investors, FAANG stocks define the market. To me, as a conservative investor, it is not. For market-cap ETFs such as SPY, FAANG has more weight than other stocks. As a group, FAANG has been very profitable for the last year. To me they seem to be risky today. The following tables summarize these stocks, and I'll check them again in a year and/or after September (usually the worst month) to confirm my findings. It is also a case of momentum vs. value.

All the info is available free on websites such as Finviz.com. All data is from 8/5/2017. These are for info only and I'm not liable for any errors. Returns are annualized and dividends are not included.

Stocks	Current Price 8/5/17	From 8/5/16 to 8/7/17	From 8/7/17 to 8/7/18	From 8/7/18 to 10/7/18	From 01/03/22 to 1/03/23
FB (Meta)	169.62	37%	7%	-84%	-63%
AMZN	173.85	29%	88%	2%	-50%
AAPL	156.39	48%	30%	48%	-31%
NFLX	180.27	48%	94%	-4%	-51%
GOOGL	945.79	17%	33%	-47%	-39%
Avg.[1]	247.41	44%	50%	-17%	-47%
Beat SPY by		214%[2]	233%	-440%	-130%
SPY		14%	15%	5%	-20%

[1] All averages in this article are estimates. Fees and dividends are not included.
[2] Beat = (44% - 14%) /14=214%. Similar to other calculations for "Beat".

From the above and assuming using the recommended trailing stops, you should have exited your positions of FAANG before 2022 and saved the loss of about 50% in 2022.

Fundamentals as of 8/5/2017 (recommend to do the same analysis whether they good buys now.

Stocks	P/E	P/E	P/S	P/B	Debt/	Sales	EPS	ROE

		FWD			Eq.	Q/Q	Q/Q	
FB	37	26	15	7	0.00	45	69	23
AMZN	16	14	6	4	1.11	2	18	27
AAPL	18	15	4	6	0.73	5	10	35
NFLX	221	90	8	25	1.55	32	58	13
GOOGL	34	24	7	4	0.03	21	-28	14
Avg.	65	34	8	9	0.68	21	25	22
Beat SPY [1]	164%		277%	186%				
SPY[2]	25		2	3				

[1] Very rough estimates.
[2] Most fundamental metrics are from other sources than Finviz.com, so there may be small discrepancies.

Technical as of 8/5/2017

Stocks	SMA50%	SMA200%	RSI(14)	52-week height	Short%	Insider Trans.
FB	8%	23%	67	-3%	1%	-86%
AMZN[1]	35%	8%	51	-6%	1%	0%
AAPL	5%	17%	63	-2%	1%	-31%
NFLX	10%	26%	59	-6%	6%	-69%
GOOGL[2]	-2%	8%	41	-6%	0%	0%
Avg.	11%	16%	56	-5%	2%	-37%
Beat [3] SPY by	1020%	173%	-9%			

[1] Recent double top. Bearish.
[2] Multiple tops.
[3] Very rough estimates.
The two SMA (Simple Moving Averages) technical metrics are positive.

Summary
As a group, FAANG is fundamentally unsound but technically sound compared to SPY. I said the same about the market. As suggested, use trailing stops if you own any of these stocks. When they turn to be technically unsound, this is the time to exit. They could stay in the current valuations for a long time. However, when the institutional investors are dumping them, they will fall very fast and steep. SMA-20% would be a good indicator for an exit. NFLX is the most fundamentally unsound stock.

The rosy pictures of these stocks have been priced in. I recommend that you sell the stocks with a P/E over 35 unless you have a good reason not to. It is insurance to protect your profits. Even if they still rocket higher, you still will have a good sleep.

9 Ukraine impact

We need to wear two hats: one for humanity and one for investing. My first hat does not like wars and the second one likes wars or prepares for wars as an investor. They are contractionary. If you feel guilty, donate your loot (from investing) to charities specific for your clause for humanity.

"2/12/2022" is one of my best days in investing. S&P 500 was down by 1.9% and I was up by 1.2% in my on-line statement of my main broker. It is a difference of 3.1%. I did not trade the markets according to the supply of metals such as nickel that affects electric car productions. As an investor, I hope it happens more often. Also I closed some of my shorts with better prices in another broker account.. The performance is due to several factors.

• Contra ETFs. It is a bright day, but most are still losing. Lesson: Only buy contra ETFs when the market timing indicator (such as the Death Cross and the Golden Cross) indicates so.

• Gold and silver. They are used to hedge inflation. Wars usually trigger the rise. Even without wars, I recommend investing about 5 to 10% in these commodities. I had almost total losses of OIL (an ETF) but good gains on USO.

• Oil and energy stocks. I have been accumulating many oil stocks recently. My screens told me they were good buys. In this case, Forward P/E is a better metric than P/E.

• Most of my recent stocks selected were based on value, and they have been doing better than the market. I have none (from my memory) of those high-flying tech stocks such as Facebook. Earnings of many global companies will suffer from global economies especially those who have to with draw their operations in Russia; if it happens to them in China, there will lead to huge losses.

• With the war dragging on, hyperinflation will continue, especially in energy and food. Many poor in developing countries have been suffering most.

Everyone should have a plan. Investing is a guessing game, and do not expect that it always works to your expectation. I am not liable for your actions. Consult your investing advisor before you invest.

Winners and losers. The U.S. will gain a lot at least initially. The EU would side with us. The EU will import more expensive oil and gas from us instead of from Russia; the Nord Stream II would have financial problems. Our defense industry sector would gain a lot of sales. Inflation starting with oil prices would be another problem for us. Our USD should appreciate when some money from Europe flows to USD. However, many countries including China that are not friendly with us may dump USD and our US treasuries. Hence, our USD as a reserve currency will be shaken.

Floods of refugees would be another headache for the EU; currently most went to Poland. Russian currency has lost about 30% in the first week. Many lives have been lost and many have been suffering in Ukraine.

China is a winner if there will not be a sanction on China for helping Russia. Russia will increase trade with China for no other better options. Taiwan should be afraid, as there is no major military help to Ukraine in case of invasion from China. We have driven Russia closer to China, shaken USD's status as a reserve currency, sped up inflation and deteriorated our relationships with many countries including EU.

By March, 1, 2022, the war seemed like it would drag on. Here are what ETFs we should buy from the date and the performances one month later.

Symbol	Description	1 M	3 M	6 M	9 M
		4/1/22	6/1/22	9/1/22	12/1/22
DBA	Agriculture	1%	2%	-5%	-7%
FXE	Contra Euro	-1%	-5%	-11%	-6%
GLD	Gold	2%	-5%	-13%	-8%
PPA	Aero + Defense	-1%	-6%	-8%	3%
UNG	US Natural Gas	24%	84%	97%	29%
USO	US Oil	3%	19%	-1%	-2%
XLE	Energy	8%	24%	10%	27%

Average		5%	16%	10%	5%
SPY		5%	-5%	-8%	-5%

I cannot find an ETF dedicated to defense. You can buy a basket of defense stocks and ignore the airline stocks that can be found in PPA. We can also short an ETF on the EU rather than shorting the Euro (using FXE in this portfolio just for convenience). The first month performs the same as SPY (the market to most), and hence you can start the portfolio a month later.

From the above, besides LNG, USO and XLE, all other ETFs turn negative after 6 months. Using trailing stops could let you exit from losing money. You can also use market timing (Death Cross) for ETFs to exit. However, even if you stay in the above portfolio for 9 months, you still beat SPY by a good margin.

#Filler: A joke I heard

The Chinese burned paper cars to their dead folks. The shopkeeper told his customer who bought a paper iPhone not to forget to buy a paper charger. It would be worse if your ancestor asked him to bring it down to his ancestor. This joke may not work for different cultures.

The customer said that his grandfather may not know how to use the iPhone. The shopkeeper told him not to worry as Steve Jobs was there to help him.

10   The changing world order

Ray Dalio, a famous investor, has the theme of "The changing world order" in his YouTube video and his corresponding book.
https://www.youtube.com/watch?v=xguam0TKMw8

The Ukraine invasion is speeding up the process. However, I believe it will take a long time for China to overtake us especially in GDP per capita; hopefully the day is not in my lifetime as I and my children are living in the U.S., and it would adversely affect our lifestyle. Let me argue on both scenario and hope we do not let our dumb nationalism cover judgement.

Dalio outlines the hints of China taking over us and let me comment on these with my own hints while some have been discussed in this book.

- Education. Obviously Chinese students are academically far better than the U.S. students as evidenced by the uniform test scores by many organizations, especially on science and technology. If you believe the extra hours of our students playing video games can compete with students of other countries not doing so, you believe in miracles. However, the U.S. is still far ahead in higher education. and that explains why we have so many foreign students including China today. We encourage creativity and are shown by our high-tech companies such as Facebook and Google.
We attract the best brains from the entire world including China. Unfortunately, our government limits foreign students from China on the grounds of security. These politicians are short-sighted as many Chinese students want to settle down in the U.S. for a better living standard and better opportunities for their children; they have contributed to our research and the economy. Hopefully we will not limit students from India, as most of them do not want to return to India as the opportunities and living standard back home are far inferior than the U.S.
Besides the obvious STEM (technical fields), our students and citizens are less civil than our previous generations. The evidence is in the high crime rate, the murder rate and constant shootings. Many enjoy our generous welfare and benefits. If you

can collect more benefits by not working, why should you work? Our gun control should be tightened.

- Technology. It is helped by the education and the research grants from the government in addition to the hard work of the Chinese. Stealing our IP is a thing of the past, and it is similar to how we stole Germany's technology after WW2 and many other examples. We have laws to protect personal privacy and hence it slows down many applications such as AI. We have moral considerations to limit our research on stem cells and drugs. Most likely, new drugs are produced in foreign countries such as China, as it is too expensive to develop them here.

  China is closing the gap in the number and quality of the research papers and grants. China leads us in many sectors in technology such as 5G, AI applications, high-speed trains, electronic payment, etc. Once they fix the fabrication of computer chips (due to our sanctions), we may lose our chip industry by the cheap chips from China. It will take at least 2 years.

- Reserve currency. USD is depreciating due to our excessive printing of the USD. Many countries are abandoning it. Saudi Arabia and Iran accept Chinese Yuan for trading and Petro Dollar is instantly dead by their decisions. The sanction on Russia's Ruble and excluding them from SWIFT are hitting our foot more than on Russia. BRICK may form their own SWIFT system. The West has found out now the importance of Russia's economy as they found out the hard way.

  The "One Belt, One Road" trades would make China's Yuan for trading, although as of 2022, USD is still the majority currency for international trades. But, it is changing fast. The sanctions make many countries worry about the chance of suffering the same fate Ruble is facing. They would cut down USD in the reserve currency partly due to the high inflation in the U.S. (i.e., the purchase power of their reserve funds in USD is depreciating). The rich folks in a country similar to Russia would fear their assets and USD would be seized if there is a conflict between their country and the U.S. I did not expect our great country would do such stupid act.

- High inflation. Besides the Ukraine war, the pandemic, our government has to face high inflation. As of 4/2022, we have 8.5% based on the latest report of CPI. It would get worse in the coming months due to the contract with longshoremen negotiation and the lockdown of Shanghai that would affect the supply chain. The lack of truck drivers and workers is another problem. The impact on the poor is higher than the rich. Ukraine and Russia are major countries to export wheat and we will feel the pain when Russia cuts down fertilizer to us. Europe depends about 40% of energy and a lot of precious ores from Russia.

- Manufacturing. We have to protect our workers, our environment, etc. Hence, we cannot compete with the cheap labor from foreign countries. Globalization solves some problems but the poor in the U.S. depending on manufacturing suffer. Hence, bringing manufacturing back home is not feasible as a $20 wage can never compete with a $2 wage. Moving factories to low-wage countries is not a perfect solution. To illustrate, an iPhone needs thousands of parts and they are supplied by many Chinese companies today, where most of them are in close proximity to the iPhone factory. In addition, these poor countries do not care about the environment and they are not rich enough to buy our products. Basically most of them are similar to China 20 or 30 years ago. Some Chinese factories have been moved there due to high-rising salaries in China.

- Trade. To me, it is not an important factor for us. We are self-supplied and do not need a lot from foreign countries. China is just the opposite. They need oil and gas, and many minerals.

- Military. We are the strongest in the world with many foreign military bases. The high cost does not justify our national security and our economy except for the defense military. Our advanced weapons can make one-sided wars with Iran and many Middle East countries, but not with Russia and China that could promote a nuclear war. If we cut down these expenses after the Afghan, we could have balanced our budget. Deploying our fleet in the China Seas is a fast way of burning money. Our carriers could be sitting ducks facing the hypersonic missiles that cannot be defended as of today.

Even with the above, I still believe we are still #1 in many fields if #1 is important to you. If we cooperate with China, we can share the technologies (that would achieve carbon neutrality by at least 2 years) and their low-cost labor to rebuild our infrastructure. I am optimistic due to our high share of resources and farmland per capita and the possible cut in our defense expenditures.

11   Winners as of 3/21/2022

I would like to find out the common characteristics of my winners, and that would help me to spot future winners in the current market. They are my current positions from my major taxable account and my son's and they are all recent buys.

At first, I wanted to include more losers, as I can learn more from the losers that I try to avoid in the future. I can only find one big loser. There is a good chance I have sold the losers already to offset my short-term gains from my short account. From my memory, they are a few big losers.

Stocks	Bought	Return	My Score	Screen
AA	11/21	97%	37	Fid
AMPY	01/22	70%	22	BG
COP	10/21	40%	35	PG
DVN	11/21	43%	44	PG
GTE	02/22	54%		
MOS	03/21	112%	15	Fid
TMST	01/22	47%	38	Ford
Loser:				
CPIX	12/21	-46%		

The other winners are: AEL 23%, BY 11%, RBB 26% and STXB 19%; COPX 11%, HBP 28% from my son's account. I have some losers with a loss of less than 10%.

Explanation:
- Sector is important. AA, MOS and TMST belong to the commodity sector while AMPY, COP, DVN and GTE belong to the energy sector. I have not used the top-down approach, but the screens selected them for me.
- My passing score (a sum of selected metrics with weights) for the long term is 15. MOS made it as it had a high short-term score. I did not have a full analysis, as I felt it was a good buy by looking at the forward P/E. I did not find a score of CPIX that I could have avoided if I did a full evaluation. My full evaluation is about 15 minutes per stock by plugging the

numbers from Finviz, Fidelity and a subscribed service to get a score.

- Two screens (Fid and Ford) are from my modified screens from Fidelity; for some reason they are not in my recent, top performers in my screens, that belong to BG. BG (described briefly in some of my books) and PG are modified screens from a subscribed service.

- The above is a review of the performance of screens, and there should be another one to review the performances of the metrics such as P/E.

Filler

I got a call from Buffett asking me to lead their stock research.
I asked him why for a nobody like me. No kidding.

He told me that he should have read my book Scoring Stocks to buy Apple instead of IBM in May, 2013. It would save his company millions of dollars minus $10 for my book. Not to mention the market timing technique that had worked in the last two major market plunges.

I told him, "OK, I'll beat your mediocre returns of the last 5 years."
He said, "You can do better than that and at least beat SPY. If you do so, no one will be that stupid to leave my fund and pay the hefty capital gain taxes."

I told him, "I cannot beat the market as you are the market especially after your expensive fees. In addition, I do not know how to avoid day traders from riding my wagon In trading. Also most of my big profits were made in small stocks that your fund cannot trade besides owning the company."

I woke up trembling. I'm glad it is only a nightmare.

12   Missing opportunities

We all have missed many trading opportunities. We learn and do not miss them in the future. Here are some recent examples. It seems we still profit after a few days when it happens. However, not all news can translate to profits.

- ASML. With the trade war with China, I noticed this company and it is the only company that produces high-end chips for Apple and Huawei. I did not take any action. The annualized return from 1/3/2020 to 1/3/2022 is 84% (SPY is 24%).

- FXI, an ETF for Chinese stocks. I believe in the long run Chinese stocks would do well. However, with the trade war and the possible delisting of many Chinese companies, we should stay away and the annualized return from the above period is -8% (SPY is 24%). I owned this loser.

- BABA, Alibaba. When the P/E was less than 3 on 3/15/21 and was less than $100 per share. I did bought some. Update: As of 4/1/2022, it is over $100 per share.

- MRNA, Moderna with the vaccines for this pandemic. The return from 1/3/2020 to 1/3/2022 is 1,144% (SPY is 24%) or 571% annualized . It is having wide rides with daily fluctuations of more than 5% many times. I did bought some shares. Pfizer did not perform well, as they did not own the intelligent property of the vaccine.

- Ukraine. Tesla could be affected by the supply of Russia's nickel for the battery. The price of the commodity of nickel has been skyrocketing. I did bought an aluminum company (AA) about 1 year ago due to inflation considerations. It was one of my best performers so far.

Ukraine's economy is being ruined, so is Russia and our corporations in Russia such as McDonald's and Visa. The U.S. farm companies and natural gas companies may make good profits by exporting them to Europe. The economies in EU will suffer from the expensive energy imported from places other than Russia. The status of our reserve currency is being shaken. China could gain a lot if there is no sanction for helping Russia. As of 3/2022, India is a winner with the cheap oil import from Russia.

13   Performances of my short-term recommendations

Some of my performances have been described. The following are from my recommendations in my book Series of "Best stocks", which were available in mid December and may be followed by an updated version in mid July; it is not a promise for future books in the series.

Book #1: "Best Stocks to Buy for July, 2021"

Start date: 07/15/2021. End date: 12/01/2021.

Momentum (2 stocks)

Symbol	Return 1 M	Ann.	Ret. 2 M	Ann
CLAR	-3%	-30%	-2%	-13%
CROX	27%	303%	33%	193%
Average	12%	137%	15%	90%
RSP	3%	37%	3%	17%
Beat RSP by	265%		440%	

Short selling betting the stocks to go down (3 stocks).

 Short selling is not recommended particularly for beginners due to the extra risk.

Symbol	Return 1 M	Ann.	Ret. 2 M	Ann
CCL	-4%	-44%	-6%	-33%
NCLH	-1%	-8%	-3%	-15%
MILE	38%	435%	45%	264%
Average	11%	128%	12%	72%
RSP	3%	37%	2%	17%
Beat RSP by	241%		330%	

CCL and NCLN are cruise liners and this sector did not perform well in this period. For diversification, you should only trade one stock in this sector.

Book #2: "Best Stocks for 2021 2ⁿᵈ Edition"
Start date: 02/08/2021 (the publish date). End date: 12/01/2021.

Momentum (7 stocks)

Symbol	Return	Ann.
ATGE	-6%	-68%
ATRS	-11%	-134%
CMRE	15%	182%
REGI	-26%	-318%
RIO	0%	-1%
SPWH	0%	-1%
WIRE	8%	96%
Average	-3%	-35%
RSP	4%	-50%
Beat RSP by	-170%	

Short selling betting the stocks to go down (3 stocks).

Symbol	Return	Ann.
HYLN	16%	191%
NEXT	2%	332%
RMO	40%	482%
Average	28%	335%
RSP	4%	50%
Beat RSP by	573%	

14   Miscellaneous strategies

- Some **mutual funds** have been losing a lot of money such as during the internet crash in 2000. Buy those funds (usually sector funds) that you expect them to recover. It could be a tax strategy as they will not distribute profits to their fund owners for a while.
- **Inflation**. They are gold (GLD, gold mines such as RING as an ETF and gold coins / bars) and silver. I prefer skipping copper and other commodities including oil unless the economy is trending up. Bonds and CDs are most likely not good investments as they return you with cash that have been depreciated due to inflation.
- Supply and demand. In 2009 and 2020, the Fed printed a lot of money excessively to save the economy. In the long run, our national debts increase. In addition, it could cause inflation unless the economy recovers due to the simulation as in 2009. There is a lot of money chasing fixed assets such as gold and stocks. As a result, both of these assets would likely rise especially in the short term. If we have hyperinflation, we would lose the buying power after cashing in the appreciated stocks.
- Almost **day trading**. When the stock is rising in the morning, there is a better chance it would continue the trend and vice versa. Reverse the trade at around 3 pm, and day traders almost never leave their positions open during weekends and/holidays. The chance is improved if both the market and the sector the stock is in are both rising. Take advantage of institutional investors. When they trade, they need days and even weeks to trade a stock. You can tell from the volume of the trade and usually the stock belongs to blue chips. Join the wagon.
- As stated before, some strategies described in this book work better than the others in different conditions of the market. If you can match the right strategy or strategies, you will see fireworks, and vice versa.
- Innovative sectors. I would skip space travel after the accident. https://www.youtube.com/watch?v=LI1hMX8qtHg
- Index rebalancing. The index such as S&P 500 rebalances at least once a year and some do it 4 times a year. If you buy the stock before it is added to the index, you should make a lot of money. The ETFs that follow the specific index are forced to buy the stocks just added to the index and sell the stocks that have been

removed from the index. I do not recommend shorting these stocks, which is risky especially for beginners.

Some indexes provide the criteria to rebalance. Here is my summary from what I guess. It is based on market cap, number of shares floating, the average trading volume (3 to 6 months), how long it has been in the market, profit (better with rising), sales (better with increasing) and any restrictions (such as a foreign stock). There are minor criteria.

Most of us do not have inside information on how any index is rebalanced. However, I tested a strategy based on the above criteria on S&P 500 for example. First criteria are the stocks should not be in the index already. So far, the testing has been proved profitable, but the test is too limited.

There are several articles that you can find via Google by entering "Index Rebalance".

The Russell 3000 index consists of 3,000 largest stocks (large cap + mid cap + small cap), the Russell 2000 index consists of 2,000 largest stocks (large cap + mid Cap), and the Russell 1000 consists of the 1,000 largest stocks (large cap). Most ETFs simulated these indexes are cap-weighted, so these ETFs do not really represent the index. To illustrate, if the ETF wants to simulate micro-cap stocks, you need to find one that is not cap-weighed and/or not including the mid-cap and large-cap stocks.

- Guru's mistakes. On 4/2021, I had too many contra ETFs betting the market to go down. It did not work due to the excessive supply of USD. I should have followed the market timing such as SMA-400 and/or death cross described in my books. However, if you buy contra ETFs in early 5/2021, you could have made very good money. Shamelessly I assume myself as a 'guru'. There are many similar examples. One analyst shorted the financial services. It did not work initially and he was fired. If the fund let him stay, he could make a lot of money.

- Positioning strategy. Start with two ETFs: SPY (or any ETF that simulates the market) and a money market ETF for example with even positions (i.e., 50% invested in each ETF). At the end of a period (a week or a month depending on how much time you have for investing), reallocate the ETFs as a percentage of how much each ETF gains (i.e., the higher allocation for the winner). For better performance, use more ETFs such adding QQQ, GLD, SH (contra ETF to SPY) and PSQ (contra ETF to QQQ).

- Buy stocks which are 95% (or 100%) close to 52-week highs. I use Finviz's Screener. To limit the number of screened stocks, I would select NASDAQ for exchange, USA for country and SMA-20 crossed SMA-50. Need to evaluate individual stock. Stop loss and market timing are important as evidenced in 2000.
- If the SMA-50 is above the SMA-100 (both available from Finviz), the stock is considered to be in an uptrend, else down trend. It is safer to use an ETF. Again, use stop orders to protect your trade. I recommend keeping the cash in the down trend instead of shorting. Use at least one more technical indicator to confirm your decision. If you start testing from 2000, you would avoid some losses from the two market crashes (2000 and 2008).
- Follow the rocket. In 2020, they are FAANG. In 2021, they are GME and AMC. The geniuses are those who follow the uptrend, and the losers are those who do not have an exit strategy such as trailing stops reviewed every week.
- Market neutral. If you think you are a better investor than others and do not want to time the market, buy a few stocks (say 3) and short sell the same number. Review your performance periodically. If you are a specialist on a specific sector, buy or short that sector periodically. Buy companies when a technology (or a drug) shows promise. The current example is AI in early 2023.
- Guru's mistakes. More than one time, a guru was fired due to betting big on a certain theme, and after a while, his predictions turned out to be correct. We have to evaluate his 'bad', and they could be at fault in time and they could turn out to be gems.
- Combine your strategy with market timing. When the market is down, short stocks using your short strategy for stocks, or buy contra ETFs using your strategy for sectors, countries or stock indexes. When the market is up, close all shorts and buy momentum stocks.
- When the market fluctuates as indicated by the market timer with false signals for example, buy stocks when the market is down and vice versa.
- Simon's strategies in using math.
  https://www.youtube.com/watch?v=cm7kkHtZiJA
- Carry Trade: Borrow a million (if they trust you) from the Bank of Japan. Buy U.S. high-yield bonds and sell them after a year or so. It works when the USD appreciates against Japanese Yen during that period, and the U.S. interest rate is higher than Japan's. I mentioned it for the last 20 years. It worked until recently.
- Most of our strategies buy on momentum and sell when the momentum is reversed. Here is one opposite strategy: buy on increasing value (from fundamental metrics such as P/E), and sell on decreasing value. The trading could be in multiple trades. The logic is the institutional investors switch sectors, and you make profit by steps

ahead of them. It worked in 2021, when the tech sector was switched to retail, and then back to the tech sector. It will not work if the sector stays in momentum for longer periods such as years.

https://www.youtube.com/watch?v=MFVmEcRHpnk&t=332s

15   More info from Fidelity

Besides Finviz, I get the EV/EBITDA from Yahoo!Finance under the Statistics tab. This chapter describes more metrics from Fidelity. The described three sites have duplicated metrics.

It all starts from "News & Research" tab. "Markets & Sectors" gives you a glimpse, and includes many related articles and insights. Fidelity's Screener can also be accessed.

We can build our income stream and CD ladder based on the info from "Fixed Income, Bonds and CDs". "ETFs" is recommended for beginners and investors who have limited time for investing.

"Stocks" will be described here in more detail. The Home page gives you a lot of general information. Try it out feature by feature.

It also gives you virtually everything about the stock. To illustrate, I enter AAPL on "Enter a symbol". Equity Summary Score is useful to me. It used to give a 5-year average of P/E. "

"Analysis and Sentiment" determine whether the stock is undervalued (good for long-term holding" or short-term sentiment (good for short-term holding).

"Analyst Opinions & Reports" typically has two reports and even more. Read them before taking any investment decision – start with high StarMine Relative Accuracy first. Some reports have more than 5-year values for specific metrics. Balance Sheet and Income Statement are also available.

Strategy 5: Sectors in a market cycle

Here are the favorable sectors in different phases of a market cycle. Here is my suggestion:

Market Phase	Favorable		Unfavorable
Early Recovery	Financial, Technology, Industrial		Energy, Telecom, Utilities
Up	Technology, Industrial, Housing		
Peak	Mineral, Health Care, Energy, Long-Term Bond, Consumer Discretionary		
Bottom	Consumer Staples, Utilities		Consumer Discretionary, Technology, Industrial, Long-Term & high-yield Bond

The sectors that cause the recession usually take longer time to recover. In 2000, the technology sector was not favorable in the Early Recovery phase, contrary to the above table. In 2007, the financial sector was not favorable in the Early Recovery phase. These are the "offending" sectors that cause the plunges.

In a recession, we usually cannot cut down on consumer staples and utilities, but we can cut down buying consumer gadgets. Companies usually postpone investing in equipment and systems during a recession and expand when the economy is humming.

All the description in Section I and III apply here. The next chapter describes the market cycle and how I define he phases of a market cycle.

#Filler: Why the market rises in 2019
The year before the election has been profitable for the market since WW2. The president wants to print a rosy picture.
First the corporate tax has been cut deeply and it makes the corporate rise. Secondly, the interest rate has been maintained very low. It stimulates the economy, especially the housing sector. It also encourages buy-back to make the stock look better. However, it may not work in the long term.

1   Market cycle

"Bull markets are born on pessimism, grow on skepticism, mature on optimism, and die on euphoria" - Sir John Templeton

The stock market has cycles as our practical interpretation of the above. It is about five years apart, but it fluctuates widely. I divide it into four stages: Bottom, Early Recovery, Up and Peak.

My defined four stages of a market cycle

We need to apply the right investing strategies to each of the four stages of the cycle.

* **Bottom**

  I would not invest for at least the first six months (or even a year) after the big plunge starts, which could lose over 25% in a few months. The exceptions are investing in contra ETFs and selling short for aggressive investors.

  I estimate it will take a year from the start of the plunge to the bottom, so I will normally sell stocks early in the plunge and do not buy stocks that are in the sector (sometimes sectors) that cause the bubble for about two years after the plunge.

  At the bottom, the high-yield corporate bonds (i.e., junk bonds) would prosper when the interest rate is decreasing to stimulate the economy.

  From mid-2007 to mid-2008, bonds suffered as the investors thought the sky was falling down - it was to those who lost their jobs and/or their houses. After that, some bonds, especially the long-term bonds, could appreciate about 50% in the following year.

  The government lowered the interest rates and these bond prices with high interest rates surged. Correct timing in buying bonds could be very profitable.

Long-term bonds have more impact by the interest rate: The lower the interest rate, the higher the bond prices of higher-yield bonds. The older bonds with higher interest rates are more valuable to the newer bonds with lower interest rates.

I define this period of the bottom from the start of the plunge to the start of Early Recovery.

- **Early Recovery**
It usually starts after one year from the plunge; no one can pinpoint the exact time consistently. By this time preferably earlier, we should have closed out all positions in contra ETFs and shorts.

Roughly speaking, October, 2007 (some use 2008) is the start of the market plunge. March, 2009 is the end of the bottom stage and the start of the early recovery stage of the 2007 cycle. However, every market cycle is different in where it starts and ends.

The one-year gain from the bottom is most profitable. It usually gains over 25% in a year from the market bottom. I, a conservative investor, had huge gains using some leverage in my largest taxable account in 2009. From my memory, I had a similar return in 2003 but I had not saved the statement as in 2009.

In this phase, value is a better parameter than growth in searching for stocks. If your investment subscription provides a composite value score and a composite timing score, the sort parameter of your screened stocks could be "Composite Value / Composite Timing" in descending order. Select the top stocks in this order. You still have to analyze the top-screened stocks.

Forward (same as Expected) P/E is a good metric. However, most companies may be losing money at this stage. Those companies that can last for more than one year with its cash reserve are potential good buys. The best appreciated stocks are beaten companies that have precious technologies and good customer bases. They could be candidates to be acquired if they are small enough.

- **Up**
  Usually, the growth metrics such as PEG could be better than the value metrics such as expected P/E during this phase. Most stocks are winners except contra ETFs and shorting stocks. When the growth stocks are making headlines and the defensive stocks are being dumped, this is the hint that we're well into the Up phase of the market cycle.

  Locate stocks with growth metrics such as favorable PEG and high SMA-200% (from Finviz.com). Do not be scared of how much they have already appreciated. The strategy "Buy High and Sell Higher" works in this phase. Protect your profits with stops.

  Ensure that they have value too. Skip the stocks with expected P/Es higher than 35 unless there are good reasons. Most stocks will gain due to the tide of the market. However, when they're overbought (RSI(14) over 65), be careful. When institutional investors sell these stocks, they will crash.

- **Peak**
  When everyone makes easy money and the interest rates are high, watch out. Stop loss and/or stop limit should be used to protect your investment. Check out whether there is any bubble that would burst like the internet in 2000 and finance (and housing) in 2007.

  The internet crisis is easy to spot, but not the financial crisis. In 2007 we had a cycle longer than the average which is about 5 years. The plunge is very fast and very steep – thanks to the institutional investors who drive the market down.

  Run the technical analysis chart described in the Chapter on Spotting Big Market Plunges at least monthly (weekly if you have time). Protect your investment. Do not fall in love with any stock (you can buy it back later at a deep discount). Making the last buck is a fool's game.

  Accumulate cash according to your risk tolerance. A retiree or a conservative investor would accumulate from 25% to 50% and should be ready to move to all cash when the plunge starts.

We can lower the cash percent if we use enough stop loss protection. Be psychologically prepared because the stock market may still rise for a while. There is no perfect market timing.

The 2007 Cycle
The market plunged starting in 10-2007 and ending in 3-2009 (bottom), started to recover in 3-2009 (early recovery), and trended up from 2010 to 1-2013 (the up phase of the market cycle). As of 3/2016, it is the peak phase defined by me.

As of 1/2013, we have recovered all the market losses since 2007. However, as of 7/2014, the economy has not fully recovered compared to the economy before the plunge. The employment judging by the medium salary has not fully recovered and the economy is not expanding. It is uncommon that the economy does not follow the market. It is due to the excessive supply of money by the government and partly due to globalization to allow companies to hire overseas.

Although a W-shaped recession seldom happens, we have a chance today. We hope we do not have a depression and/or the similar lost decades that Japan has been experiencing. Some may conclude we are close to completing a market cycle from 2007 to 2016. As of 2016, the economy is recovering slowly and we're better than most other global economies.

Again, market timing is not an exact science as it involves irrational human beings and government interventions. The timing using the market cycle described here is a guideline as it is hard to time it exactly.

The average market cycle is about 5 years, but they fluctuate. If we consider 2007 as the plunge, we have about 8 years of this cycle as of 2015.

In a typical cycle (few are typical), we have about one year in each of the 4 phases I defined (plunge, early recovery, up and peak).

Events/Triggers

There are financial events and triggers that cause the transition of one phase of the market cycle to another. They usually do not change the sequence of the phases (say not from Peak to Early Recovery), but they may change the duration of the phase. Examples are:

- The government announcing change of the interest rate,
- Change of employment, and
- Change of GNP.

Sectors in a market cycle (my suggestion)

Market Phase	Favorable		Unfavorable
Early Recovery	Financial, Technology, Industrial		Energy, Telecom, Utilities
Up	Technology, Industrial, Housing		
Peak	Mineral, Health Care, Energy, Long-Term Bond, Consumer Discretionary		
Bottom	Consumer Staples, Utilities		Consumer Discretionary, Technology, Industrial, Long-Term & high-yield Bond

The sectors that cause the recession usually take a longer time to recover. In 2000, the technology sector was not favorable in the Early Recovery phase, contrary to the above table. In 2007, the financial sector was not favorable in the Early Recovery phase. These are the "offending" sectors that cause the plunges.

In a recession, we usually cannot cut down on consumer staples and utilities, but we can cut down on buying consumer gadgets. Companies usually postpone investing in equipment and systems during a recession and expand when the economy is humming. The government usually lowers the interest rates right after the plunge to stimulate the economy.

Conclusion

When the market is about to plunge or change from one stage to another, run the described chart more frequently and read more articles written by the experts.

Again, market timing is not an exact science but it is based on educated guesses. The better guesses should have more rights than wrongs in the long term. Our actions depend on our risk tolerance. Be careful of using any new strategy that has not been fully understood and proven. Since 2000, market timing is very important to your financial health with two market plunges with an average of about 45% loss.

Afterthoughts
- The Dow Theory has a lot of followers in detecting market directions. In a nutshell, the market heading upwards is confirmed by the Industrial Index and the Transportation Index (less important in today's market especially with internet sales such as songs and movies), and vice versa. As of 4/2014, the two indexes are not in uniform.
  http://finance.yahoo.com/blogs/talking-numbers/this-is-a-130-year-old-warning-sign-for-stocks-231901097.html

  - The bear market has the following three phases.
  1. The market is overvalued.
  2. Corporations are not doing well with decreasing earnings and sales.
  3. Investors are selling due to fears.

  It is the reverse for a bull market: 1.The market is under-valued. 2. The market increases due to increasing corporate profits/sales and 3. Investors are buying due to greed.
- Investopedia has several articles on this topic.
  http://www.investopedia.com/terms/b/businesscycle.asp
- The yield curve could predict the interest rates change and hence the economy. There are three main types of yield curve shapes: normal, flat and inverted.

A normal yield curve is one in which longer maturity bonds have a higher yield. Similarly, the long-term CD should have a higher interest rate than the short-term CD.

When the shorter-term yields are higher than the longer-term yields, it indicates an upcoming recession. A flat yield curve indicates the economy is transiting. Now, you've read the essence of a book on this topic costing about $50 to buy.

However, especially today, it does not mean anything as the government supplies too much money to stimulate the economy unsuccessfully. My simple chart described using SMA-350 (Simple Moving Average for 350 trading sessions) which depends on the stock price works better. Click here for "The dynamic yield curve" (http://stockcharts.com/freecharts/yieldcurve.php).

The interest rate plays a role too. The easy money encourages folks to borrow money to buy stocks and companies to acquire other companies.

- As of Feb., 2013, I believe we're in the Up stage of the market cycle. I checked the performances of my top screens from each stage (a.k.a. phase) of the market cycle for the last 60 days. The best performance as a group belongs to the screens for the Up stage. Controversial! Always use the screens (same as searches) that perform well recently.

In addition, the market has recovered 120% of the loss of 2007-2008. Hence the duration for an average Up stage of the market is quite close.

- Total Market Cap / GNP ratio is hotly debated on the market value. Different from the traditional 100%, I would suggest that the boundary ratio should be 130%. If it is over 130%, the market is overvalued and vice versa.
  http://www.investopedia.com/terms/m/marketcapgdp.asp
  Market cycle:
  https://www.youtube.com/watch?v=ebWL2TrIssA
  Bull market:
  https://www.investopedia.com/terms/b/bullmarket.asp

Bull / Bear market

This is a summary of my views. In short, most investments appreciate in a bull market, and vice versa in a bear market. It is indicated by the described Golden Cross and Death Cross. In 2022's bear market, even the bonds did not fare well. It is partly due to raising the interest rates too fast to counter inflation. If inflation is under control, the Fed would not have another interest hike.

The market cycle is usually ahead of the economy cycle. When conditions such as low interest rates, companies make easy money and hence boost the general economy. When the economy is overheated, the Federal Reserve has to increase interest rates to cool down the economy and prevent the formation of a bubble. At that time, most companies suffer and lay off workers. At the end of this cycle, the Federal Reserve most likely lowers the interest rates to stimulate the economy and start the cycle again.

Investors should be very careful in investing during the bear market and avoid failing companies. In the beginning of the bull market, invest in companies that their stock prices have been beaten up but have a good chance to survive. Many S&P 500 companies were formed during the bear market. The lack of venture capital is offset by lower expenses and fewer competitions.

#Filler: Destruction of a country

Is the membership of NATO worth the destruction of a country? Definitely not. A good politician should get the membership before his announcement. Murdering citizens is a war crime to me.

2 Profitable Early Recovery

I had an 80% return in 2009 in my largest taxable account. I did not include it in my other books before as I just found the statement. Early Recovery, a phase of the market cycle defined by me, is the best time to make a profit. My chart told me to start to move to equity in September, 2009. I did in March, 2009 for other reasons. It could be luck, technique or both.

I did dip into the credit line of my equity loan (not recommended to most) due to lower interest rates than a margin interest. I paid back the loan right after I sold some stocks. The turnaround was high until I exhausted my short-term losses (tax loss harvest). The strategy is bottom fishing. Some sectors described are better in this stage of the market cycle.

I had similar success in 2003. I did not have a defined bottom fishing technique at that time. I expected the market to fully recover in two years. From Value Line, I selected stocks with high "Projected 3–5-year returns" and the short-term assets can last for two more years (judged by the burnt rates).

As the stocks are recovering earnings (E), the trailing P/E may not be a good indicator, but the Forward P/E may be. Most sites on evaluating stocks such as Fidelity have a value grade. Also look for candidates for acquisition. From the last recoveries, I spotted at least one such candidate. They are usually small companies (50 to 300M market cap) and have valuable assets such as customer base and patents. Aggressive investors should buy stocks with the worst timing grades and this the only time to do so; these beaten-up stocks could be big winners.

An article stated that the entire company of an internet company can fit into the conference room of Exxon, and it had the same market cap as Exxon if my memory serves me right. In early April, 2000, I switched all my tech mutual funds in my annuity into traditional sectors (better to cash in hindsight) to avoid the crash. Fishing in the market bottom is risky but very profitable. The Golden Cross could miss the bottom as it depends on past data. Other hints are Buy / Sell ratio is less than 0.2, RSI(14) for SPY is less than 25 and the market has more than 40% lower from the peak.

The stocks that have been beaten down badly and have poor timing scores could be the stocks that have the highest appreciation potential. It is different from the traditional evaluation. I prefer those stocks with positive earnings or at least not losing a lot. The appreciation periods for most of these stocks may not last long. Hence, I recommend using trailing stops (and reviewing the stops periodically) for appreciating stocks. To illustrate, you do not want to lose more than 10% from the peak of a stock and do not take profit prematurely.

My predictions for 2023. If the market recovers in 2023, it could be the beginning of a new cycle. We can use the market timing indicator to confirm it. If there is a serious recession, all bets would be off.

I invested a lot of defensive stocks such as consumer staples, healthcare and utilities. The stocks I recommended in 79% or my book "Best stocks for 2022" has a return of 4% beating RSP by 153% from Dec. 15, 2021 to Dec. 1, 2022. Not counting market timing and the acquired USAK that gained 79% and annualized to 105%.

http://tonyp4idea.blogspot.com/2022/12/best-stocks-series.html

During market recovery, usually the beat-up stocks recover first. Usually the small stocks gain larger profit in the short term and then the large caps. Ensure the stocks are profitable or at least Forward P/E is positive.

Links:
Bottom fishing:
https://www.youtube.com/watch?v=hANAn9szRBA
Recommended stocks for Q3 2022. Understand why.
https://www.youtube.com/watch?v=4lxS7pfGukM

3   A turnaround strategy for value stocks

Many value stocks tend to stay in this phase for a long time. When the turnaround starts, it could be very profitable.

Market Timing
Do not buy any stock when the market is risky as described elsewhere in the book. Actually, you should sell most of the stocks when the market is risky.

Metrics

Metric	Value	Conservative	Aggressive
General			
Market Cap	>300 M	>1,000 M	>100 M
Price	> 2	>10	>1
Avg. Volume	>20,000	>50,000	>10,000
USA	Only	Only	Foreign but listed in USA

Fundamental			
Forward P/E	<15	<10	<25
Earning Gr Q-Q	>5%	>8%	>3%
ROE	>10	>15	>5
P / FCF	<10	<8	<15
Debt / Equity	<.5	<.25	<1
Technical			
SMA-50%	>10	>15	>5
Misc.			
Blue Chip Growth	A or B	A	A or B
Fidelity	>6	>8	>5
IBD	>60	>90	>50
VectorVest	>=1	>=0.8	>=12
Value Line Proj. 3-5% return	>5%	>10%	>5%
Zacks	>=4	5	>=4
ASSS	>=2	>=5	>=2

The assignment values for the metrics are not fixed; feel free to change it according to your own risk level. I do have suggestions for conservative investors and aggressive investors. Some of the metrics are not readily available in Finviz.com and the following describes how to modify them.

Explanation

- Market Cap- The free version of Finviz.com does not allow you to specify the range. Use 'Any' and then select the stocks according to the specified values. Average Volume has a similar restriction.

- The conservative values for Market Cap, Price and Average Volume try to select larger companies. The aggressive values try to select smaller companies, which historically are riskier but perform better.

- I prefer 'USA' for Country. Stay away from small companies from developing countries unless you can trust their financial statements.

- Forward P/E measures the value of the stock. Ensure "E" (Earnings) is positive. I prefer it over P/E (from the last twelve months).

- Earnings Growth Quarter to last Quarter is preferred to be positive unless it is during a recession.

- ROE measures how well the company has been managed.

- P/FCF. "Price / Free Cash Flow" cannot be manipulated easily. Together with low "Debt / Equity", it measures whether the company would go bankrupt.

- SMA-50%- Some stocks tend to stay in a value stage for a long while (termed value trap). We like to select stocks that start getting out of this stage.

- Misc. Many sites have evaluated the stocks for us. Some only let their customers access such information, some are available for a free trial, or are available from the library.

- ASSS is my scoring system. Try it out and check the performance. With the above, I had 35 stocks on 10/28/16 and that was too many stocks to evaluate. If you have time for 10 stocks for further evaluation, try to sort Forward P/E (P/E is the second choice) in ascending order and select the top 10 after skipping the stocks that have P/E less than 2. If you cannot find any or substantially less than the normal, the stocks you selected may not work, take a break as the market conditions do not favor the value metrics you specified.

Qualitative analysis

Double click on the stock and read as many articles described on the stock as possible. If it meets all the criteria, buy the stock. I recommend that you use market orders for large companies in a non-volatile market (when the average daily fluctuation is less than 0.5%). If the selected stock is the one you just sold for a loss, make sure you only buy it back after 31 days to avoid the Wash Sale penalty.

Keeping informed

Check the company updates/news on the stock you owned every month. One easy way is to enter the stocks in a model portfolio in SeekingAlpha.com and they would inform you on any articles/news on your owned stocks.

Sell the stock

Re-evaluate your stocks every 6 months. If it does not meet the criteria or the market is risky, sell it. If it is only a few days (currently it is 365) away from a long-term capital gain, sell the losers right away or hold on to the winners for a few more days.

Rebalance the portfolio after a stock has been sold. Ensure it has been diversified enough into market cap and sectors.

Top-down Investing

It is similar to the above. Find the sectors that performed the best last month. Under Finviz.com, select the best sector under 'sector' one at a time. Several sites such as Fidelity compare a stock to the averages of stocks in the same sector.

My recent recommended stocks being delisted

There should be more of these stocks when the market recovers from crashes. From my last books in my "Best Stocks" series, which are verifiable, my shares are quite a lot. Again, fees, dividends and commissions are not included,

Stock	Rec. Date	Date delisted	Days held	Return	Ann. Return
USAK	12/15/21	09/14/22	273	79%	105%
BDSI	12/15/21	03/22/22	97	116%	436%
CTB	02/08/21	06/17/22	129	15%	41%
Average			71	70%	194%

#Filler: The best health hint

Buy a lottery ticket as early as possible before a big payout. The good feeling of the potential making millions could be the best medicine money can buy.

4   Bottom fishing

This could be risky but very profitable, particularly during Early Recovery (a state of the market defined by me and can be detected using Golden Cross). I used it several times and it has been proven successful to me. Here are the common characteristics, and some can be found in Finviz.

- Beaten up. The Perf Year is more than -50% (i.e., its share price has lost more than 50%).
- Fundamental Rating from many sites such as Fidelity (preferred over Finviz) is below average.
- Timing Rating is below average.
- Forward Earnings Yield (1 / (Forward P/E) is positive. If it is not positive, check out whether the company can survive in two years (cash available / burn rate for 2 years).
- Stock Price > 1.
- Market Cap > 100 M.
- It is in one of the major indexes such as S&P 500, S&P 600 (mid cap) and Russell 2000 (small cap).

I prefer:
- Positive insider buying.
- Positive institution buying.
- Low Debt/Equity.
- Positive Q-Q Sales growth.
- Positive Q-Q Earnings growth.
- No major lawsuits.

Acquire candidates (with technology and/or market share of the specific areas).

5   Market timing by calendar

The following predictions are based on historical data. You may have slightly different findings depending on when you start and when you end your testing.

You can load the historical data of SPY via Yahoo!Finance and check out how close you are or different from my own predictions. They are my predictions based on historical data. Use it as a reference only.

- Presidential cycle.
  Usually, the market performs worse in the first two years after the election than the next two. During the **3rd year** the president has to make the economy look rosy in order to buy votes. Statistically it is the best year for the market and is followed by a good year (the election year). The government may stimulate the economy, the stock market and employment by printing more money, lowering interest rates and lowering taxes. The market in the 100 days before the election should be positive and less volatile according to 40 years of data. The next 100 days after the inauguration should be good for the market (termed as the honeymoon period).

  Democratic presidents have better market performance statistically than Republican presidents. This is not too logical as though Republicans are more pro-business traditionally.

- Olympics.
  It has been proven that the host country has a better chance that its stock market appreciates the year after the Olympics. It could be due to the exposure from the Olympics and / or the huge expenses in preparing for the Olympics.

  The last two Olympics follow this pattern as of 12/23/2013:

Olympics Country / Year	ETF	Period	Return
United Kingdom / 2012	EWU	Jan. 3, 2013 - Dec. 23,2013	11%
China / 2008	FXI	Jan. 3, 2009 - Dec. 31, 2009	43%

Greece could be an exception. It is too small a country to host this world-class event and it has wasted too many resources by building too many white elephants that the country can never justify. Brazil depends on its export of natural resources to China, so I do not count on the Olympics effect there. Japan 2020 was adversely affected by the pandemic.

Winning a lot of Olympic medals has no prediction for the stock markets. Both the Russian Empire and E. Germany were winners but disappeared in their original forms afterwards.

- Seasonal.
  Best profitable investment period is: Nov. 1 to April 30 of the following year. It is similar to the saying 'Sell in May and Go away'. It has not worked since 2009 as it was an Early Recovery (defined by me) in the market cycle.

  The market does not always happen as predicted. However, when more folks follow this, it becomes a self-fulfilling prophecy. I prefer "Sell on April 15 and come back on Oct. 15" to act before the herd. The more practical strategy is to start selling on April 1 and become more aggressive (selling at closer to the market prices) when it is close to May 1. For the last five years, I did not find this prediction reliable.

  The explanation of the 'summer doldrums' could be that the investors cash their stocks for vacations and college tuition in the fall. Buying quality companies at the dips could be profitable.

- The worst month: September.
  The next worst month is October. However, if there is no serious market crash during October (and this month has more than its shares of crashes), it could be the best month to buy stocks.

- The best month for the bull: November.
  However, several market bottoms occurred in October and November. The next strong month is December.

- Best 30 days: Dec. 15 to Jan. 15, next year.
  It was correct for the period of 2012-2013.

- Window dressing.
  Institutional investors sell their losers and buy winners around Nov. 1. From my rough estimate and on the average, the winners have a 2% percentage point gain better than the market and the losers have 1% worse than the market.

  I recommend that you evaluate the top 10 winners from the last 10 months or YTD on Oct. 15 and sell them at 3% gain or two months later.

  I recommend that you buy in Dec. and sell them 3 months later. Include the stocks with more than 30% loss for the last 11 months or YTD, sort them by Earning Yield in descending order and evaluate the top 10 stocks.

  In both cases, do not buy foreign stocks and stocks with return of capital. Ignore stocks not in the three major exchanges, with low volumes and stock prices less than $2. Do not buy in losing years such as 2007 and 2008. I have my tests with my own assumptions and I use tools not available to most readers.

This is a guideline only. Do not buy any stocks during market plunges. Current events should be considered first such as a potential war and the hiking of interest rates.

Afterthoughts

- I predict it will be a sideways market in the later part of 2013. I am following the sideways strategy: Buy on dips and sell when the market is up. One's prediction.
- Why September has a bad reputation?
  http://www.marketwatch.com/story/betting-on-septembers-terrible-odds-2013-08-27?dist=beforebell

September of 2013 (2 days away at the time of this writing) may have more problems. Check out how many of the following are correct on Oc. 1, 2013. Use it as a future guideline to predict the next September using the current market conditions then:

1. The market is not excessively expensive, but it is not cheap. It is due for a 5% correction.

2. Unrest in Syria (check any unrest in your next prediction in September).
3. High oil prices due to Syria.
4. September is statistically a bad month for the stock market. However, it could be an opportunity to invest after the correction if any.
5. Interest rates are rising.
6. All the above indicate the market will dip. However, the rosier outlook is that the global economies are improving even slowly.

- January effect.
  The performance of January may determine how the entire year performs. I cannot find any rationale but it has been proven right statistically.
- Earnings period announced in Jan., April, July and Oct. would cause big swings in stocks when they have surprises. Earning revisions could be a good predictor.
  http://www.investopedia.com/terms/e/earningsseason.asp

Links
Presidential Cycle:
http://www.investopedia.com/articles/financial-theory/08/presidential-election-cycle.asp
Calendar-based market timing:
http://stock-chartist.com/2010/10/calendar-based-market-timing/
Calendar market timing for 2013:
http://www.investorecho.com/archives/8047

Filler: The problems of the U.S.

1. Our political system. We waste time arguing between the two parties. There is no long-term planning, as the other party could claim the credit. Same as corporations' CEOs who care about their yearly bonuses.
2. The politicians have to satisfy their voters. Today give them free cash by jacking up the printing press. And ignore the long-term consequences.
3. We have to protect our workers, our environment... Hence, we cannot compete with many countries.
4. We have spent too much on military and ignore our crumpling infrastructure.
5. Historically no country can rule the world forever.
6. We blame China, but ignore how hard-working Chinese are.

Appendix 1 – All my books

Book	No. of Pages	Link	ebook
Art of investing 5th Edition	570	Click here	link
Sector Rotation: 21 strategies 5th Edition	525	Click here	Link
Be a stock expert in 5 minutes. Expanded Edition.	203	Click here	Link
Using Finviz 5th Edition	570	Click here	Link
Using Fidelity 5th Edition	570	Click here	Link
Momentum Investing 3rd Edition	285	Click here	Link
Using profitable investing sites	500	Click here	link
Investing successes and plunders	415	Click here	Link
Best stocks to buy for 2025	375	Click here	Link

If you already have my book that is over 300 pages, most likely you do not need to buy the above books except the "Best Stock" series, which may be available every December – not a promise.

For paper-bag readers, access the links via the following link.
https://www.blogger.com/blog/post/edit/7608574268453692676/1786802320953936467

Most books have paperbacks. Links and offers are subject to change without notice.

Best stocks to buy for 2025

The current book is "Best stocks for 2025" in this series.

https://www.amazon.com/dp/B0D2459JDT

If the sales of my books in this series were based on past performances, I should have sold many books, but obviously not.

Book	Stocks	Return[3]	Ann.	Beat RSP by[1]
Best stocks to buy for 2024	8	46%	48%	132%
Best stocks to buy for 2023	8	36%	36%	290%
Best stocks to buy for 2022	10[6]	4%	4%	153%[7]
Best Stocks to buy as of July, 2021[4]	8	5%	13%	487%
Best Stocks for 2021 2nd Edition	10	42%[4]	52%	220%
Best Stocks for 2021	4	29%	44%	118%
Best Stocks to Buy from Aug, 2020	14	45%	45%	3%[5]
Avg.	9	34%	40%	208%[2]

Here is the detail:
https://tonyp4idea.blogspot.com/2024/12/best-stocks-to-buy-for-2025.html

---

Sector Rotation: 21 Strategies 5th Edition

- On 5/26/2020, I searched for "Sector Rotation" under Amazon's Book. They are listed in the same order except my book Sector Rotation: 21 Strategies.

Book	Date	Size[1]	Kindle $[1]	Hard $
Sector Rotation: 21 Strategies	05/2020	425	$9.95	$24.95
Super Sectors	09/2010	289	$26.39	$49.95
Dual Momentum Investing	11/2014	240	$40.40	$42.20
Sector Investing	05/1996	260		$29.94
Sector Trading Strategies	08/2007	164	$26.39	$16.66
The Sector Strategist	03/2012	225	$26.39	$44.96
ETF Rotation	10/2012	125	$9.95	$14.99
Optimal... Sector Rotation	07/2015	80		$44.07

[1] From Amazon on size and prices as of 5/25/2020.

My book won in all categories except the price for hard copy in one. However, my book won as the lowest cost per page by a wide margin. In addition, as of 5/2020 I bet that no author besides me made over 4 times using sector rotation starting the amount more than his yearly salary then.

- I have **21** strategies in sector rotation while most books have only one. It ranges from simple rotation of a stock ETF and cash for beginners to many advanced strategies for experts. Most other books have one or two strategies.
- Andrew, a contributor on Sector Rotation article at Seeking Alpha, said, "Great stuff, Tony. It's great to meet experienced traders such as yourself. I had a browse through the book and think your method is a little more refined than mine."
- "You have written the book in a way that makes good and logical sense." Bill.
- Do not be fooled by past performances. Just check the recent performance of the top 50 stocks selected by IBD in the last five years. The mediocre result (hopefully it will change) could be due to too many followers and/or there is no evergreen strategy. I seldom heard the fantastic results from the followers of O'Neil, our greatest chartist. The adaptive strategy of this book shows you how to select the most profitable strategy for the current market.
- I switched most (if not all) my sector funds in April, 2000 from technology sectors to traditional sectors (better to money market fund). We can reduce losses by spotting market plunges and the sector trend.

Shorting Stocks and ETFs

Recent performances.

Stocks	Short Date	Close date	Duration	Return	Annualized
ACVA	06/10/21	09/29/21	111	22%	72%
CCL	07/14/21	09/29/21	77	-8%	-36%
CENX	09/17/21	09/29/21	12	3%	105%
CLOV	09/16/21	09/29/21	13	10%	291%
CSPR	09/16/21	09/29/21	13	33%	917%
EOSE	09/15/21	09/29/21	14	10%	261%
MILE	07/22/21	09/29/21	69	53%	279%
NCLH	07/27/21	09/29/21	64	-5%	-27%
REAL	06/04/21	09/29/21	117	22%	68%
UAVS	06/04/21	09/29/21	117	41%	127%
Average	07/30/21	09/29/21	61	18%	206%
RSP	S&P 500			0%	

It is for education purposes and I am not responsible for any errors. As in most parts of this book, commissions, dividends and fees (interest for shorts) are not included, and hence the returns are less than specified. They are real and all trades for the period.

Stocks	Short Date	Close date	Duration	Return	Annualized
BBIG[1]	09/30/21	11/19/21[1]	50	35%	258%
BFLY	09/30/21	11/18/21	49	14%	107%
EOLS	11/10/21	11/17/21	7	10%	523%
FLDM	10/13/21	11/18/21	36	14%	147%

MKFG	10/27/21	11/18/21	22	-9%	-149%
PAVM[1]	10/20/21	11/19/21[1]	30	34%	413%
TSP	10/05/21	11/18/21	44	-11%	-91%
VRM	10/13/21	11/17/21	35	13%	135%
Average	10/14/21	11/18/21	34	13%	168%
RSP	S&P 500			4%	

Appendix 2 – Art of Investing

Art of Investing 5th Edition consisting of 15 books in 1. Besides saving money and your digital shelve space, it gives you quick reference and concentration on the topic you're currently interested in. It covers most investing topics in investing excluding speculative investing such as currency trading and day trading. It has over 550 pages (6*9), about the size of two investing books of average size.

The 15 books

Book No.	Amazon.com
1	Simple techniques
2	Finding Stocks
3	Evaluating Stocks
4	Scoring Stocks
5	Trading Stocks
6	Market Timing
7	Strategies
8	Sector Rotation
9	Insider Trading
10	Penny Stocks & Micro Cap
11	Momentum Investing
12	Dividend Investing
13	Technical Analysis
14	Investing Ideas
15	Buffettology

The book links are subject to change without notice.

"How to be a billionaire" is for beginners and couch potatoes, who can use the advanced features of this book in the simplest and less time-consuming techniques. Most advance users can skip this section unless they want to use some of the short cuts described.

We start with the basic books Finding Stocks, Evaluate Stocks, Trading Stocks and Market Timing. You can select and start with one of the many styles and strategies in investing such as swing trading and top-down strategy. Many tools are described in other books such as ETFs, technical analysis, covered calls and trading plan.

Many books start with "Why" to lure you to read more and are followed by "How" and then the theory behind the book.
If the book you're reading is beneficial to you, imagine how it would with 850 pages.

Most readers' comments are on "Debunk the Myths in Investing", which this book is originally based on. As of 2018, I did not know any of the commentators on my books.

"I skipped ahead to his chapter book 14 (of "Complete the Art of Investing"), Investment Advice just to get a feel of his writing style. His research is phenomenal and doesn't overwhelm with big words or catchy "sales-like" tactics.

I truly believe this ordinary man, Mr. Tony Pow, has a gift of explaining his experience as an investor without the bull crap of trying to make you buy his stuff. He seemingly just wants to share his knowledge, tips, and clarity of definitions for the kind of folks like me who want to understand something FIRST before jumping in with emotions of trying to make a boat load of money. I like the technical analysis side he brings.

Mr. Tony Pow talks about hidden gems in his book; well....quite frankly, he is a hidden gem. Thank you and I will also post my comments about this author to my Facebook page!" – JB on this book.

"Excellent book, recommend to all investors... great knowledge. It has fine-tuned my investing strategies... Your book is hard to set aside, as I read it all the time learning good techniques and analysis of stocks, ETF... Since I purchased your book in March, I have underlined, highlighted and placed tabs on top of pages for quick reference." – Aileron on this book.

"Tony, I just finished reading your 2nd edition. It's my pleasure to report that I found it most interesting. You're welcome to use this blurb if you like:

Debunk the Myths in Investing is an all-encompassing look at not only the most salient factors influencing markets and investors, but also a from-the-trenches look at many of the misconceptions and mistakes too many investors make. Reading this book may save not only time and aggravation but money as well!"

Joseph Shaefer, CEO, Stanford Wealth Management LLC.

"Tony, Great work!" from James and Chris, who are portfolio managers.

"'Debunk the Myths in Investing' is a comprehensive book on investing that deals with many aspects of this tense profession in which with a lot of knowledge and a bit of luck (or vice versa) one can greatly benefit...

Therefore 'Debunk the Myths in Investing' is an interesting book that on its 500 pages offer a lot of knowledge related to investing world and many practical advice, so I can recommend its reading if you're interested in this topic."
- Denis Vukosav, Top 500 Reviewers at Amazon.com.

"490 pages (Debunk) of a genius's ranting and hypothesis with various theories throughout, written light-heartedly with ample doses of humor...Yes, the myth of not being able to profitably time the market is BUSTED...

One might ask... Why is he giving away the results of his hard-earned research for only $20? He states that his children are not interested in investing and wants to share his efforts with the world." - Abe Agoda.

"Excellent book, recommend to all investors… great knowledge. It has fine-tuned my investing strategies… Your book is hard to set aside, as I read it all the time learning good techniques and analysis of stocks, ETF… Since I purchased your book in March, I have underlined, highlighted and placed tabs on top of pages for quick reference." - Aileron on this book.

"Great stuff, Tony. It's great to meet experienced traders such as yourself. I had a browse through the book and think your method is a little more refined than mine."
"Your strategy is very rules based and solid. I sometimes envy people who have developed something like this."

Making 50% in one month

I claim to have the best one-month performance ever for recommending 8 or more stocks without using options and leverage. My following return is 57% in a month or 621% annualized. They are slightly different as I calculated the average from the averages of three different accounts. The average buy date is 12/26/18 and the "current date" is 01/28/19.

The performance may not be repeated. I will use the same screen for the coming years and even the expected 10% (or 120% annualized) is very good.

I used the same screen for searching stock candidates. I spent a total of about 20 hours from Dec. 15, 2018 to Jan. 5, 2019.

Stock	Buy Price	Sold or Current Price	Buy date	Sold or Current date	Profit %	Profit % Ann.	Status
CHK	2.13	2.99	01/03/09	01/18/19	40%	982%	Sold
MNK	16.41	21.45	01/03/19	01/25/19	31%	510%	Sold
MNK	16.43	21.45	01/03/19	01/25/19	31%	507%	Sold
NNBR	5.68	8.58	12/26/18	01/28/19	51%	565%	
NNBR	5.72	8.58	12/26/18	01/28/19	66%	727%	
ESTE	4.35	6.45	12/26/18	01/18/19	48%	766%	Sold
LCI	4.61	8.29	12/21/18	01/28/19	80%	767%	
MDR	8.01	9.13	01/08/19	01/28/19	14%	255%	
YRCW	3.29	5.78	12/21/18	01/28/19	76%	727%	
YRCW	3.26	5.78	12/21/18	01/28/19	77%	742%	
ASRT	3.56	4.18	12/26/18	01/28/19	17%	193%	
UTCC	7.13	11.00	12/26/18	01/28/19	54%	600%	
YRCW	2.92	5.78	12/26/18	01/28/19	98%	1083%	

Best one-year return

I claim to have the best-performed article in Seeking Alpha history, an investing site, for recommending 15 or more stocks in one year after the publish date without using options and leverage.

https://seekingalpha.com/article/1095671-amazing-returns-velti-alcatel-lucent-alpha-natural-resources

Appendix 3 - Our window to the investing world

The paperback version of this chapter can be found in the following link.
http://ebmyth.blogspot.com/2013/11/web-sites.html

- **General**
  Wikipedia / Investopedia /Yahoo!Finance / MarketWatch / Cnnfn / Morningstar /CNBC / Bloomberg / WSJ / Barron's / Motley Fool / TheStreet
- **Evaluate stocks**
  Finviz / SeekingAlpha / MSN Money / Zacks / Daily Finance / ADR / Fidelity / Earnings Impact / OpenInsider / NYSE / NASDAQ / SEC / SEC for 10K and 10Q (quarterly) reports required to file for listed stocks in major exchanges.
- **Charts**
  BigCharts / FreeStockCharts / StockCharts /
- **Screens**
  Yahoo!Finance / Finviz / CNBC / Morningstar /
- **Besides stocks**
  123Jump / Hoover's Online / FINRA Bond Market Data / REIT / Commodity Futures / Option Industry
- **Vendors**
  AAII / Zacks / IBD / GuruFocus / VectorVest / Fidelity / Interactive Brokers / Merrill Lynch /
- **Economy.**
  Econday / EcoconStats / Federal Reserve / Economist /
- **Misc.**
  Dow Jones Indices / Russell / Wilshire / IRS / Wikinvest / ETF Database / ETF Trends / Nolo (estate planning) / AARP /

Appendix 4 - ETFs / Mutual Funds

What is an ETF
ETFs have basic differences from mutual funds: 1. Lower management expenses, 2. Trade ETFs same as stocks, and 3. Usually more diversified but not more selective than the related mutual funds such as NOBL vs FRDPX.

The major classifications of ETFs are 1. Simulating an index such as SPY, QQQ and DIA, 2. Simulating a sector such as XLE and SOXX, 3. Simulating an asset class such as GLD and SLV, 4. Simulating a country or a group of countries such as EWC and FXI, 5. Managed by a manager(s) such as ARKK, 6. Betting a market or sector to go down such as SH and PSQ, and 7. Leveraged (not recommended for beginners).
Fidelity: Index ETFs (https://www.fidelity.com/etfs/overview).
Wikipedia on ETF (http://en.wikipedia.org/wiki/Exchange-traded fund).

List of ETFs
ETF database (Recommended): http://etfdb.com/
ETF Bloomberg: http://www.bloomberg.com/markets/etfs/
ETF Trends: http://www.etftrends.com/
A list of ETFs. Seeking Alpha.
http://etf.stock-encyclopedia.com/category/)
A list of contra ETFs (or bear ETFs)
http://www.tradermike.net/inverse-short-etfs-bearish-etf-funds/
Misc.: ETFGuide, ETFReplay
Fidelity low-cost index funds:
https://www.youtube.com/watch?v=zpKi4_IJvlY
Fidelity Annuity funds with performance data.
http://fundresearch.fidelity.com/annuities/category-performance-annual-total-returns-quarterly/FPRAI?refann=005
ETFs vs mutual funds;
https://www.youtube.com/watch?v=Vmz0CzlQvHk
Three ETFs: https://www.youtube.com/watch?v=MVi2RhpffuU

Other resources
Most subscription services offer research on ETFs. IBD has a strategy dedicated to ETFs and so does AAII to name a couple. Seeking Alpha has extensive resources for ETF including an ETF screener and investing ideas. So is ETFdb.

Not all ETFs are created equal
Check their performances and their expenses.

When to use or not to use ETFs
I prefer sector mutual funds in some industries, as they have many bad stocks such as drug industry, banks, miners and insurers. Most mutual funds cannot time the market.

When you believe a sector is heading up (or contra ETF for heading down), but you do not have time to do research on specific stocks, buy an ETF for the sector; it is same for the market.

Half ETF
Taking out half of the stocks that score below the average in an index ETF could beat the same full ETF itself. I call it HETF (half the ETF). You heard it here first.

To illustrate, sort the expected P/E (not including stocks with negative earnings) in ascending order and only include the stocks on the first half. Add more fundamental metrics. It will take a few minutes.

Disadvantages of ETFs
- When you have two stocks in a sector ETF one good one and one bad one, the ETF treats them the same. Stock pickers would buy the one that has a better appreciation potential.
- Sometimes the return could be misleading due to stock rotation. To illustrate this, on August 29, 2012, SHLD was replaced by LYB in a sector fund. SHLD was down by 4% and LYB was up by 4% primarily due to the switch. Unless you sell and buy at the right time (which is impossible), your return would not match the ETF's returns due to the replacement.
- Ensure the performance matches the corresponding index; it is hard due to excluding dividends.

Advantages of ETFs
- We have demonstrated that you can beat the market by using market timing. Between 2000 and Nov., 2013, you only exit and reenter the market 3 times and the result is astonishing.

- It is easy to rotate a sector vs. buying/selling all of the stocks in this sector. Rotating a sector is the same as trading a stock.
- The risk is spread out, and your portfolio is diversified especially for a market ETF or buying three or more ETFs in different sectors.
- Periodically the bad stocks in most funds are replaced by better stocks.
- Eliminate the time in researching stocks.

Leveraged ETFs

I do not recommend them. Some are 2x, 3x and even higher. They're too risky for beginners. However, when you are very sure or your tested strategy has very low drawdown, you may want to use them to improve performance. Most leveraged ETFs and contra ETFs have higher fees.

My basic ETF tables

I include some contra ETFs, mutual funds and Fidelity's annuity. Some of these may be interesting to you. Most Vanguard's ETFs have lower fees.

ETFs and funds come and go. Some ideas and classifications are my own interpretation. Refer to ETFdb for updated information. Not responsible for any error. Check out the ETF or fund before you take any action.

I prefer VFINX over SPY for the lower fees; both simulate the S&P 500 index. The stocks in the ETF can be either equally weighted or weighted by market caps. The latter is more like using momentum strategy, as the rising stocks usually have larger market caps. The index usually kicks out some poor-performing stocks and replaced them with better stocks. These ETFs are suited for long-term investing without constant reviews.

Table by market cap:

Category	ETF	Mutual Funds	Fidelity's Annuity	Contra ETF	Alternate
Size:					
Large Cap	DIA			DOG	
	SPY			SH	VOO VFINX RSP FXAIX
	QQQ			PSQ	FNCMX

	RYH				
Blend	IWD	BEQGX			
Growth	SPYG	FBGRX			FSPGX
Value	SPYV	DOGGX			FLCOX
Dividend	NOBL	FRDPX			
	VYM				
Mid Cap			FNBSC	MYY	
Blend	MDY	VSEQX			
Growth		STDIX			
		BPTRX			
Value		FSMVX			
Small Cap			FPRGC	SBB	FSSNX
Blend	IWM	HDPSX			
Growth		PRDSX			FECGX
Value		SKSEX			FISVX
Micro	IWC				
Multi					
Blend		VDEOX			
Growth		VHCOX			
Value		TCLCX			
Total					FSKAX VTI
Bond					
Long Term (20)	VLV	BTTTX		TBF	
Mid Term (7 – 10)	VCIT	FSTGX			
Short Term (1 – 3 yrs.)	VCSH	THOPX			
Total	BOND	PONDX			
Corp Invest Grade	VCIT	NTHEX			
High Yield (junk)	PHB	SPHIX			
Muni	MUB	Check state			
Special situation					
Buy back	PKW				

Table by sectors:

Sector	ETF	Mutual Funds	Fidelity's Annuity
Banking[1]		FSRBK	

Regional	IAT		
Biotech	IBB	FBIOX	
	XBI	Large	
Consumer Dis.	XLY	FSCPX	FVHAC
Consumer Staple	XLP	FDFAX	FCSAC
Finance	KIE	FIDSX	FONNC
	IYF		
Energy	XLE	FSENX	FJLLC
Energy Service		FSESX	
Gold	GLD	FSAGX	BAR
Gold Miner	GDX	VGPMX	
Health Care	IYH	FSPHX	FPDRC
	VHT	VGHCX	
House Builder	ITB	FSHOX	
	ITB	Perform	
Industrial	IYJ	FCYIX	FBALC
Material	VAW	FSDPX	GSG
	IYM		
Oil	USO		
Oil Service	OIH	FSESX	
Oil Exploration	XOP		
Real Estate	VNQ	FRIFX	FFWLC
REIT	VNQ		
Retail	RTH	FSRPX	
	XRT		
Regional bank	KRE	FSRBX	
Semi Conduct	SMH		
Software	XSW	FSCSX	
	IGV		
Technology	XLK	FSPTX	FYENC
	FDN	FBSOX	
		ROGSX	
Telecomm.	VOX	FSTCX	FVTAC
Transport	XTN		
	IYT		
Utilities	XLU	FSUTX	FKMSC
Wireless		FWRLX	

Footnote. [1] Also check Finance.

Table by countries outside the USA:

Country	ETF	Mutual Funds	Fidelity's Annuity	Alternate
Australia	EWA			
Brazil	EWZ			
Canada	EWC	FICDX		
China	FXI	FHKCX		
EAFE	EFA			
Emerging	VWO	FEMEX	FEMAC	FPADX
Europe	VGK	FIEUX		
Global	KXI	PGVFX		
Greece	GREK			
India	INDY	MINDX		
Indonesia	EIDO			
Latin America	ILF	FLATX		
Nordic		FNORX		
Hong Kong	EWH			
Japan	EWJ	FJPNX		
S. Africa	EZA			
S. Korea	EWY	MAKOX		
Singapore	EWS			
Taiwan	EWT			
	TUR			
United Kingdom	EWU			
Foreign:				
Combination				
Intern. Div.	IDV			FTIHX
Small Cap	SCZ			
Value	EFV			
Europe	VGK			

#Filler: Honey, my book can play music.
https://www.youtube.com/watch?v=HxGT5z6d-GA&list=PLMZa6mP7jZ2b1otqG4tfbgZpLEdh6YiNF

Appendix 5 - Links

The following may be repeated from the articles and it is for your convenience. To illustrate, Under YouTube (or Investopedia), search "Finviz". Some links have permanent values such as most articles from Wikipedia and Investopedia. Others reflect current events such as the current market. Learn from them and act when the current events have similar descriptions. For the printed versions, enter the following in your browser: https://tonyp4idea.blogspot.com/2023/02/links-in-my-books.html

Beginners

Common mistakes: https://www.youtube.com/watch?v=zkNueyFs8zQ

Best Vanguard ETFs https://www.youtube.com/watch?v=mSEyghlZchQ

Buy stocks/ETFs: https://www.youtube.com/watch?v=4vjkeC_4EmU

Screener

Finviz https://www.youtube.com/watch?v=cHNUMPgEYGY

Recommended YouTube: https://www.youtube.com/watch?v=CJoN7wLfWNo
PEG: http://en.wikipedia.org/wiki/PEG_ratio
Short %:
http://www.investopedia.com/university/shortselling/shortselling1.asp#axzz2LNDvpemo

Openinsider:	http://www.openinsider.com/
Finviz:	http://Finviz.com/
terms:	http://www.Finviz.com/help/screener.ashx
Insider Cow:	http://www.insidercow.com/
Current Ratio:	http://en.wikipedia.org/wiki/Current_ratio
Cash Flow:	https://www.youtube.com/watch?v=1v8hRZ36--c
Balance sheet:	https://www.youtube.com/watch?v=DZjU0CHKyV4

How to find quality stocks.
http://seekingalpha.com/article/2381395-how-to-identify-quality-stocks-and-is-there-really-alpha-to-be-had

Investing strategies

Inflation: https://www.youtube.com/watch?v=Zpthvpy3UKg\

Swing: https://www.youtube.com/watch?v=C9EQkA7uVU8
_____ https://www.youtube.com/watch?v=a_wpfSXRSjo
https://www.youtube.com/watch?v=M8sNMhPJIN

Momentum: https://www.youtube.com/watch?v=PpUlOyZrl9
Penny stocks: https://www.youtube.com/watch?v=u7xZ3kF62u4

Scanning https://www.youtube.com/watch?v=7iZpWmwBhel

Peter lynch 2023: https://www.youtube.com/watch?v=CK1AkVVVXu8

Charlie: https://www.youtube.com/watch?v=8g2B6QJ2FEc
Dividend ETFs: https://www.youtube.com/watch?v=64NEiyoNBIM

- Innovative   sectors:
  https://www.youtube.com/watch?v=LI1hMX8qtHg

Trading stocks
Beginners: https://www.youtube.com/watch?v=aod3cyUEu4k
Covered call https://www.youtube.com/watch?v=dzMOnI4Eh04

Tax Avoidance: http://en.wikipedia.org/wiki/Tax_avoidance
Tax Law: http://en.wikipedia.org/wiki/Income_tax_%28U.S.%29
Without paying (gift tax):
http://en.wikipedia.org/wiki/Gift_tax_in_the_United_States#Gift_tax_exemptions
http://www.irs.gov/Businesses/Small-Businesses-&-Self-Employed/What%27s-New---Estate-and-Gift-Tax
AMT: http://en.wikipedia.org/wiki/Alternative_minimum_tax
Estate planning fun. http://tonyp4idea.blogspot.com/2014/08/estate-planning-101-for-me.html
Taxes on stocks: https://www.youtube.com/watch?v=EKYMbsjUUtE
Tax avoidance: https://www.youtube.com/watch?v=tXou5pM7zh0
Capital gain: https://www.youtube.com/watch?v=ezPs4ibFsNU&t=2678s
Trading course: https://www.youtube.com/watch?v=8sbfrusR5Eo
How safe our brokers. https://www.youtube.com/watch?v=wz64z1YuL0A

Fidelity funds: https://www.youtube.com/watch?v=xdEunmLrhb4
Fidelity core money market fund:
https://www.youtube.com/watch?v=KU6HYRHj3jg

Government bond default? https://www.youtube.com/watch?v=wMxj6iB92ZA
Broker CDs (Recommended): https://www.youtube.com/watch?v=zhEiyW2N7KE
Money market fund: https://www.youtube.com/watch?v=N53wZ_80abU

Economy
YouTube   video   (highly   recommended):
https://www.youtube.com/watch?v=Q6NIDJZdQH4

What will the world be in 5 years (2027).
https://www.youtube.com/watch?v=LzipwDQBUyc
Inflation and interest rate:
https://www.youtube.com/watch?v=q8KJSNyAHLE
Wealth gap widens with low interest rate:
https://www.youtube.com/watch?v=t6m49vNjEGs
Investing helps the economy:
https://www.youtube.com/watch?v=W6ICRTqsxk8